LETTERS FROM INDIA

THE WRITINGS AND CORRESPONDENCE OF BERYL GIRARD, MISSIONARY

Edited with an Introduction and Commentary by
Pamela Girard

AuthorHouse™
1663 Liberty Drive
Bloomington, IN 47403
www.authorhouse.com
Phone: 1-800-839-8640

© *2010 Pamela Girard. All rights reserved.*

No part of this book may be reproduced, stored in a retrieval system, or transmitted by any means without the written permission of the author.

First published by AuthorHouse 4/21/2010

ISBN: 978-1-4520-0101-2 (e)
ISBN: 978-1-4520-0100-5 (sc)

Library of Congress Control Number: 2010904306

Printed in the United States of America
Bloomington, Indiana

This book is printed on acid-free paper.

For Al and Shirley

With thanks

Beryl Girard, 1945

Introduction

It was a hot day and muggy when I discovered the letters. I was going through the home of my mother and father-in-law to ready it for sale. It was a beautiful old home, built the early 1900's. It was filled with books, journals, antique furniture, photos, memories, and all the just-in-case things people who lived through the depression and the dust bowl days often saved.

They were in an antique walnut sofa desk. It was too hot to work any longer so I sat in the dim light and read them the rest of the afternoon. They were shared with a few members in the family who loved them as much as I. We filed them away as one does when faced with the more pressing need of selling a house and distributing all its contents among family.

The first time I met Beryl was in the summer of 1957. She was home from India on furlough. After receiving medical treatment for various parasites and tropical diseases, she attended a series of meetings, this one in Seattle.

Scott, her nephew and I, newly married, were living in a tiny one-bedroom furnished apartment while he attended Seattle Pacific University. Because transportation was provided for her, she was able to stay with us.

I remember how very small she seemed to me, tired and frail. Her dark eyes, dark hair and olive complexion, a gift of her French Canadian ancestry, were beautiful and served her well in India. She spent her leisure time trying to keep warm, Seattle's climate a big adjustment from the heat of India, drinking tea and writing letters.

She was a North Dakotan, born on a farm near Milner, a small town in the southeastern part of the state. After her mother died when she was a teenager my husband's folks, Bernard and Helen Girard, became Beryl's surrogate parents. She moved in with them to finish high school. Bernard, or B.A. as he was called, was her eldest brother. He was superintendent of schools in Scranton, North Dakota, high school teacher, and the coach of Beryl's basketball team. My husband, Scott, was born during her stay. She loved him dearly as she did all the babies in the family.

B. A. obtained a degree from the University Of North Dakota in 1928 and entered medical school. He dropped out (temporarily as it turned out) with just $3.18 in his pocket. The plains were reeling under the effects of the so called "dirty thirties." Drought was widespread.

The second eldest, Merle, studied engineering at the University, but dropped out of school for the same reason as his brother. He became a postal worker on the railroad, subsequently severely injuring his leg in a train wreck. Though one would never guess to be around him, this injury, along with bad knees, limited him in later life. He was the father of Al who, with his wife Shirley, watched over and cared for Beryl in her retirement.

The third child, Persus Nehring or Pinkie as she was called, became a nurse, married and while nursing, raised numerous children. At this writing she still lives on a ranch in western North Dakota. After her retirement Beryl would visit her as often as she could, traveling from Minneapolis in a tiny car and later on the train.

Upon completion of high school, Beryl entered Northwestern Bible College in Minnesota, studying to become a missionary. She received her degree in 1943, but due to the war in Europe there was a delay of two years before she was able to begin her mission. She was assigned to India under the auspices of the Conservative Baptist Foreign Mission Society and embarked to India in May,

1945. Her job was to work with the Kurkus, an indigenous people who had their own language.

Although Beryl learned to speak Hindi fluently as a native, her first job was to learn the language of the Kurku people which had never been written. She would sit on the ground, cross-legged with the village story teller and tape record her stories. What she learned she wrote down with all the difficulties of verbs, adjectives, subtexts, syntax and grammar. Then she translated the Gospels, wrote primers, and taught the Kurku people how to read their own language, and learn the story of Christ.

In the beginning her letters showed how isolated Beryl was. She was isolated by language, customs, culture, religion, often from her partner, the world she knew and the world at large.

They conveyed the immensity of the job she had undertaken. But gradually over the 38 years she was there, there slowly developed a community of faith, friendships, and finally of family. Her legacy is a family of God that continues to grow and expand today.

As much as she loved her family here and missed them and North Dakota, I now realize how deeply she loved India and its people.

Pamela Girard

Contents

Chapter 1 The Journey to India 1
Chapter 2 Letters to North Dakota 5
Chapter 3 Letters to Minnesota 43
Chapter 4 Letters to the World 73
Chapter 5 "So I'll Travel Along With a Friend and a Song" 95
Chapter 6 "All Creatures Great and Small" 99
Chapter 7 "Suffer the Children to Come Unto Me" 109
Chapter 8 Meditations on Scripture 121
Chapter 9 Fruits of the Spirit 129
Chapter 10 The Final Journey 133

CHAPTER I

THE JOURNEY TO INDIA

*"As My Father Hath
Sent Me Even So Send I You"*
(John 20:20)

In May, 1945 we, Ruth Ihrig, Dora Johnson and I, left New York on the Portuguese ship, S. S. Quanza bound for Lisbon. The war in Europe had just ended, but was still raging in the Pacific. We were to transfer in Lisbon to another ship that would take us around South Africa. The much shorter passage through the Suez Canal was closed. Damaged or sunken ships had not been cleared.

In Lisbon we learned that all ships at port had been taken over by the Government of Portugal. We could go no farther. So began a long wait as we and other missionaries searched for another ship.

June went by. In July we received word that a British troopship was being repaired at Gibraltar. They would take passengers going to India. We together with missionaries of the Independent Presbyterian Mission, traveled from Lisbon, through Spain and down to Gibraltar. There we were ferried out to the troopship. British troops lined the deck as we approached.

The British and Indian troops were on their way to Bombay and we would be the first ship to go through the Suez Canal. We traveled blackout and were required to keep our life belts with us at all times. We crept through the Suez where there were signs of sunken ships on either side.

We were assigned to our own area. Dora, Ruth, and Elsie Hudec, a classmate from Northwestern Bible College, and other missionaries, a woman, and a couple with four small boys ate in our private dining room.

On August 3, 1945 we slid into Bombay harbor. It had been a long trip. British customs checked us through. To my dismay my precious box of books simply could not be found. I had my first lesson, "don't worry about material things."

We were transferred to Mission Hostel and introduced to mosquito nets. We were exhausted. Ruth quickly crawled under the mosquito net, but I headed for the bathroom.

When I turned on the light, there was a very large rat facing me. I left, but when I returned he was gone. Thus began my 38 year vendetta against RATS.

Editor's notes:

On May 7, 1945, the war in Europe ended when the Germans surrendered to the Americans and to the Russians and England on May 8, 1945. They traveled just after Germany's surrender and the end of May.

The S. S. Quanza, a Portuguese ship on which she sailed in 1945, was moored in Hampton Roads, Virginia in 1940, loading coal for the return trip to Europe. 86 passengers, Jewish refugees from Nazi persecution had been denied entry into Cuba, Mexico and New York and were to return to Europe. A Jewish lawyer from Newport News, along with the help of Eleanor Roosevelt, found a loophole in our immigration laws and they were allowed into the United States.

There are three stories that circulated among our family about boarding the British ship. The first was there were so many personnel lining the deck to watch for the women, the ship listed. The second was they sang, "Oh, You Beautiful Doll" as they arrived on deck, and third, they had many marriage proposals. I suspect all three are true.

The war in the Pacific ended on August 15, 1945, two weeks after she arrived in India. Her brother Bernard, a Navy corpsman, was assigned to the Marines during the invasion of Okinawa. They were packing up to invade Japan when the war ended with the unconditional surrender of the Japanese after the atomic bombs were dropped.

Scott, Beryl's nephew and Bernard's son, heard Col. Paul Tibbets, pilot of the Enola Gay, which dropped the first atomic bomb on Hiroshima, speak shortly before his death in 2008 and bought his book. Scott, who never gets autographs, used the book signing as an excuse to thank Col. Tibbets for the life of his Dad who was able with all the others to come home.

Chapter 2

Letters to North Dakota

"My Beulah seems a long way away."
(Beryl Girard)

Ellichpur, Berrar, M.P., India
March 17, 1954

Dear Pink and all,

    I don't know where the time goes, but my notebook says I haven't written to you all for a long time, or anyone else for that matter, for my desk is piled high with unanswered mail. Good thing you don't wait for a letter before you write or I would surely be out of luck, and lonesome. Your letters do me so much good.
    After the Ramakhera mela (meeting), we started out on tour again. Ruth and Eileen took a jeep load up toward Khirkiya and I started off in a new area. The roads were terrible, through a very dense jungle. I had to return to Dharni after a couple of days to get Lilla and we got thoroughly lost that night as we returned. Pannu Master was with us and though he assured me, "I'd never let you get lost!" He wasn't a bit of help.
    We didn't realize when we began work in that new area that the Roman Catholics were already there ahead of us. They had a school and a church, but do very little evangelizing so we went

ahead anyway. While we were there, Grubbsie came out one evening bringing two of our missionaries from Japan. They were on their way home for furlough and stopped off here to see the India field. They surely saw plenty, for Grubbsie (*Mr. Grubbs, a pastor*) had never been out in the area before and they spent the day wandering around in the jungle trying to locate us. Then he left the women with us while he tried to return to Dharni alone.

We warned him, but he felt he had to get back. Anyway he got lost, nearly went over a very high cliff and ended with his car wedged up against a tree. He spent that night in the jungle. Next day he started for help on foot. He finally found a village and got a bullock cart to go back with him, also got a cup of tea. Then he couldn't find the jeep. They spent all afternoon trying to locate it. He got home late that night after two days and a night in the jungle.

Lilla and I had to take the women back to Dharni after a couple of days. We found a new road that was very good (as jungle road go), but we knew we would have a time finding our way back for there are so many trails and they all look alike. Lilla tacked up a piece of string on one tree, and as we returned, you would have laughed to see us out of the jeep examining the dust for jeep tracks. We figured we are almost as good as bloodhounds. At least we got back safe enough.

We were out nearly two weeks and it was hard for the days are awfully hot and a tent almost unbearable. Last week Ruth and I were together again touring back in the Sembadoh area. We finally ended up in Khamla too tired to do any more touring for this year.

Right now I am at Ellichpur. I am chairman of the catering committee this year which means that I have to head up all the meals for conference next week. Ruth and Pat are also on the committee, but neither one knows much about cooking. Anyway I have been getting supplies together; that involves seeing that the rice and wheat is cleaned, getting the wheat ground into flour and buying up supplies of potatoes and onions, etc. It is a big job, but we will have less than 30 this time so perhaps we can manage.

It is awfully hot, but the Ellichpur bungalow has electricity and so fans are in order – and cold drinks from the ice box, even had ice cream twice since I came down. This really is civilization for us folks from the jungle. Ruth and I are planning to stay at Khamla this year during the hot season. We have such a lot of studying to do and lessons to plan and it is the only place we can find to do work like that for it is quiet and the heat doesn't get too bad.

We got another missionary nurse into India, Ruth Lee, and an additional nurse has been granted a visa. But so far the couples coming for evangelistic work have not been allowed entry. One couple that had just returned from furlough last year are resigning and going home. Another couple had to fly home for medical treatment. Others are going home on furlough and have little hope of getting back. A lot of sickness is out here among us, but Ruth and I stay amazingly well.

Can't imagine you as ever being fat. Anyway you better not try dieting too seriously. It will wear off. Of course you could take after Aunt Addie.

Really saw the prize story of the last tour. We were sitting in a Korku house and while Astar bai was talking to all the women, I was looking around. One child of about 4 or 5 crawled into his mother's lap and nursed for a while. Then he ran out to where the men were and the next thing I knew he was back in the house sitting calmly on the floor puffing on an Indian cigarette. His mother and grandmother were right there and no one admonished him. He puffed for a while and then snuffed it out on the floor just as the men do. All the kids chew tobacco from 7 or 8 years on. They are expert at spitting between their teeth.

Laughed last night at a tiny mouse. This bungalow here at Ellichpur is full of them. Somehow I don't mind mice; it is rats I hate. Well, this wee mouse was headed for a sack of corn I had on the floor. I didn't want a hole chewed in my sack so I hissed at him. The mouse was so startled that it jumped at least 4 inches straight up in the air and lit running. Funniest thing I've seen for a long time.

I am enclosing a few pictures I got from Allen's wife and some from Merle of the baby. Maybe you have some too. Had a letter from Aunt Addie recently. Guess Art has been sick. Thought he had cancer, but the doctors at Rochester said no. They are getting old. Just got a note from Ruth wanting me to hurry back to Khamla. Says she is getting thin. I doubt that, but she really didn't have much in the line of supplies when I left. I'd better try to get the work done here as soon as possible and get back up there with some food. She really could stand to lose a pound or two though.

Love, Beryl

Editor's Note:

After India became independent of the British Empire, the government was averse to western influence. Why Beryl was allowed to return is not known.

Letters From India

Top Left: Hair washing in the Tapti River. **Top Right:** Marketing in the village. **Bottom:** Beryl on furlough with her brother Bernard. **Bottom Right**: Ruth and Beryl beside the "selfish little car".

Pamela Girard

Khamla
December 26, 1954

Dear Bernard and Helen,

Christmas time and though I did not get greetings back to you in time to say Happy Christmas, you may be sure you have all been in my thoughts. Guess it is a sign of old age to be reminiscing, but that is just what I have been doing this evening, remembering some of our Christmases together. Surely is a long time since that night back on the farm when Pinkie's and my Santa Claus' whiskers caught on fire. And I guess none of us will forget that last Christmas we were all together when Mother was still with us.

I was disappointed for a moment when I found Mother's gift to me was a Bible, for I had never been able to read past the flood. I surely didn't realize then that the Bible would change my whole life and bring me a peace and joy I had never known before. I miss the snow and the Christmas tree and the beautiful music. We have 4 records of carols and we play them over and over. Most of all I miss you.

Well, the Thursday before Christmas Ruth and I finally got packed up to leave Ramakhera for a few days rest here at Khamla. Packing up means that we tried to empty out the house for we can't be sure there will be anything left when we return. Then Ruth had a bunch of plants that had to go and the two cats had to be shut up in a pinser (small screened in cupboard we use to keep milk or vegetables in). Naturally the cats protested and the plants took up a lot of room.

But rest doesn't start when you first move into an empty bungalow. We had to sweep out all the dirt and mess left by the rats, unload, and go after water. We usually haul our water in a couple of drums in the trailer. When we got down by the well, we could see that it looked rather dampish around. I had my doubts about driving in, and sure enough I got stuck. Finally I was able to back out, and park some way from the well on dry ground. That meant we had to haul all that water by pail quite a distance (each drum holds 25 pails). The caretaker drew the water and we had to carry it to the trailer, lift it up, and dump it in the drums. Anyway, we really appreciated our warm bath that night; and if you could have seen us, you would have agreed the water was put to good use.

Christmas Day we were up early for we were going to Katkomb to spend Christmas. The road was not as bad as we had anticipated and we made the 10 miles in less than two hours. Ruth led the morning service telling the Christmas story in pictures, then going on to show the reason for our Lord's coming and the cross and resurrection. After church the men all got together to plan the evening meal. We were invited to dinner at Nu's house and the chicken curry was simply delicious. Well, in the meantime the men found that they had no chickens for the evening meal so it was decided we would have to have our Christmas dinner the next day.

After a sing that night Ruth and I spread out our bedrolls on the floor of the church and went to sleep. Next morning we all had to help get the meal ready before church. An Indian meal requires a lot of work. The men hauled a big tank of water in a bullock cart, prepared the chicken and did all the actual cooking. We women got the rice ready, that is pounded off the husks, and then picked out all the stones and weed seeds. That takes a long time. Someone had to grind the pulse for the bhajiya into flour, another had to prepare the spices. The spices are ground on a flat stone by rolling another small stone on top of them. There was a whole plateful of red peppers in the spices and the woman who ground them complained about her hands burning. Ruth is still complaining about her stomach burning for that chicken curry was delicious but oh, so hot. And now after three meals of chicken curry we have had enough for a few days.

The months of November and December were really busy ones trying to keep our Bible school going and having whooping cough at the same time. I really didn't do too much whooping except at night, but I have coughed day and night for six weeks. I don't have much trouble now, and all the sore spots have cleared up except one. Anyway Dr. Jack advised me to rest for a couple of weeks and that is why we are at Khamla. When we were packing up out in the village, I stubbed my little toe on some of our boxes and I guess I must have broken it. So I have been limping as well as whooping.

Our doctor goes on furlough in February. Already the hospital is closed for we have no other doctor to take his place. He plans to study while home so that he won't be back for a couple of years. That means we either have to use the local doctor, or if anything serious comes up, go to Bombay or Vellore (it's one of the best mission hospitals in India, but it is in south India and a long way from here).

Did I tell you about the time last hot season one of the missionaries from a neighboring mission came in to see our doctor? Naturally he was very ill or he would not have made the trip in. Our doc was gone, so Tom Major went to get the local doctor. This doctor is quite a musician it seems, and when Tom called, the doctor's wife seated him and he began to wait. Finally the doctor appeared with an Indian musical instrument in his hand. He informed Tom that there was a certain program on the radio that he always accompanied, and so Tom had to wait until the program was over before the doctor would go with him. I wonder if our family doctor *(Bernard)* pulls any such tricks on his patients. No, they could probably find him out at the city dump shooting rats – huh?

Today we watched for a few minutes a Kurku girl being tattooed. There is a big design that goes all over their forearms and it must be a very painful process. Anyway she had her eyes covered and another woman held her arm. She surely was crying. They have their own distinctive marks on their foreheads so that you can tell at a glance they are Kurkus. The Gondi women, and their jungle tribe similar to the Kurkus, have the whole back of their legs tattooed from the ankle to the thigh. They have a "V" on their forehead and their eyebrows lengthened as well as their arms tattooed. I suppose in olden days it was a protection in a time of war to be able to be identified at a glance. For all that there are so many castes in India, it is soon quite easy to identify them for they all have their own different dress and jewelry, and since they marry only within their caste, each caste looks distinctive.

Now see what a long letter I have written – don't know if you find news from here interesting or not. Well, it is too late to send Christmas greetings, but not too late to wish you all a very happy New Year. May the Lord bless you each one and may He be real and precious to you this New Year.

Love, Beryl

Editor's Notes:

The letters I found to Bernard and Helen didn't start until 1954. When Bernard returned from the Pacific after the war ended, he enrolled in medical school. He and Helen resigned from their teaching jobs and they, with their two children, moved across the state and later across the country towing a rickety home-made trailer with just the barest of necessities. Beryl's first years in India were spent learning Hindi, which she learned to speak fluently. I imagine some letters got lost along the way.

During her first furlough in 1950 she was able to see Bernard graduate from Temple University Medical School in Philadelphia, her nephew, Scott from high school and her niece Ferol from eighth grade. She also attended the graduation ceremony at Ryder College in New Jersey because Helen (after receiving a Master's Degree in English in 1946, a rarity then) was teaching there.

I believe it was this trip that required a return to India on a cattle boat that sailed around South Africa rather than through the Suez Canal. She was the only passenger not sickened by the stench.

Pamela Girard

Ramakhera, Deratalia, Nimar Dist., M.P., India
January 10, 1955

Dear Bernard, Helen, Scott and Ferol,

Your card came yesterday. I was looking for it for I can usually count on a letter Christmas time at least.

And thanks much for the very generous gift. I'm surprised you are looking or investigating other places – I thought when you built your house there you'd at last really found a place to settle down. I'll be interested to hear what develops. You must have had a nice Christmas with both Scott and Ferol LaRae home. Sorry to hear that your mother has cancer and trust the deep x-ray will fix her up.

Not too much news since I last wrote the night after Christmas. We are back in our village house – rather camping outside it, while we replaster it with the usual mixture of mud and manure. Dries slowly inside now so we won't be able to move back in for another 3 days. I've even helped apply the stuff and my hands are scraped raw and blistered here and there from rubbing the stuff over the rough walls. Believe me back on the farm I never realized or appreciated the value of cow manure. Hindus of course place great value on its cleansing merits. Always you can see folks in the city gathering it up, even following the cattle with a basket. Fuel is expensive and dung burns well.

Well, I could tell you a few other uses of the cow dung as well as urine but I guess you might not appreciate the information! Do write when you can – all the news.

Love, Beryl

Editor's note:

She kept her small home in India shining. The floor was highly polished dried cow dung and she spread braided rugs here and there. Her garden was carefully tended.

Letters From India

Dharni, Amravati Dist. M.P., India
April 2, 1956

Dear Bernard and Helen,

The calendar says it's another birthday for you, Helen. May this be a happy year for you and the Lord bless you richly.

Thanks for writing about Margaret. I could not remember her last name and so for weeks could do nothing about contacting her. Then it seemed to me their name started with a "J" and so by going through all the J's in my card file, I arrived at Jaffie. Anyway yesterday I received an answer back to my letter to her and now when we go through Calcutta April 13th on our way to Darjeeling for a vacation, I'll see her.

Yes, this year we are going to the hills for a rest. We are very tired – Ruth almost sick from the heat. There we will be able to study and concentrate once more. (There is never an end to language study.)

Well, since I last wrote we've been busy with Bible conferences. This last one I used an interpreter – that is I spoke in Hindi and one of our evangelists translated my message into Marathi. That's the first time I've ever done that and I must say I was scared – but it turned out okay.

And we had a wedding. Usually our Christian weddings are simple, but this one was very <u>fancy.</u> The wedding was set for 4:30 so we got to the church by 4 to be sure of a seat (on the floor). It was very hot and we were packed together. The bride didn't show up – so finally at 5:30, Mr. Grubbs began the sermon – without the bride.

At last she arrived and I nearly swallowed my tonsils when I saw the procession. A little flower girl strewed rose petals – the bride wore a lovely white silk sari topped by a long net veil. The train was carried by two more little girls, all in white satin and very lovely with their shining black hair and eyes. The bride wore white anklets, shoes and white gloves that looked like the canvas gloves we wore back on the farm.

She'd forgotten the bouquet so after she was seated beside the groom, someone passed up the white paper roses. They had such long stems that they were always in the way. Mr. Grubbs had malaria and felt rotten and we were all roasting, but we had to have another sermon now that the bride was there!

Finally it came time for the ring – and the bride couldn't get her glove off for the roses were still clutched tightly in one hand. Mr. Grubbs tried to help her and got those roses shoved in his face. For a moment I expected to see the bouquet go flying out the window! Well, it was finally over and we were all glad to get outside. I was looking very well myself in a new pink sari with a black border, but no one seemed to notice how beautiful I was.

We hate to see Christians go to such expense for their weddings. A lovely sari makes a beautiful wedding gown and everything else – western – seems superfluous. The Hindus go deeply into debt over their weddings, in fact, it's often the son's job to pay off his father's wedding debts and so it goes on unendingly. But it is the <u>thing to do.</u>

It's evening and at last the temperature is dropping, 89 now. I've baked bread and a lemon pie – too bad you can't join us for supper.

Love, Beryl

Editor's Notes:

When Beryl walked home from the wedding she found tiger prints – a tiger had been following her!

Beryl adopted India's dress, a sari and sandals, finding it more comfortable, cooler and practical. The dress of westerners was far too hot and cumbersome. With her long dark hair (often worn in a braid,) a tan and dark eyes, she fit in well with the people with whom she worked. Once she was on a train platform waiting for a train to Bombay a "mem sahib" (English wife) ordered her from the "whites only" section of the station. I think she was secretly pleased. It was her habit to travel third class as it gave her an opportunity to practice her Hindi and learn about her fellow passengers.

Dharni, Amravati Dist., M.P., India
July 4, 1956

Dear Bernard, Helen, Scott and Ferol,

Dating this letter reminds me that it must be a holiday back home. Right now it is pouring down rain over here and that "uster" be what happened at our Fourth of July picnics. Maybe times are changed. Guess folks don't take time to go on picnics any more.

Well, it has been so long since I have written to you or heard from you that I hardly know where to begin. We had a good holiday in Darjeeling; but as for seeing Mt. Everest, we will have to take Tenzing's *(Norgay)* word for it that it is really there. We surely didn't see it. All the time we were there we had rain and fog so that we rarely saw even the closer ranges. But it was beautiful and refreshing.

Darjeeling's population is mostly made up of Nepali and Tibetan folk. The religion of that area is Buddhism or rather Lamaism. Everything was so different from our area that we felt as though we were in a foreign land. The standard of living is much higher, also it's much cleaner. Maybe the climate has a lot to do with that.

We really were fascinated by the Tibetans. They are the cowboys of the East and it is really something to see them swagger through the street, their long coats tied around their waist by the sleeves leaving it hang like a skirt to about their knees; britches tucked into felt boots that are often beautifully decorated; long hair braided into a pigtail hanging down their back or wound around their head; broad brimmed hat; and armed with a dagger fore and a sword aft. The women are often very pretty and fair with rosy cheeks. They seem to love a joke.

Pamela Girard

We wanted terribly to see one of their mule trains as it came in loaded from Tibet and we finally did. This one was bringing in raw wool. We visited the last Indian outpost on the Tibetan trail. There were a couple of families of missionaries there in that very lonely post. One of the men said he had seen the mule trains carrying in jeeps to be assembled in Tibet. Soon there will be a road right through into India from Tibet. I would want that road well guarded if I were India.

On our way home we stopped over in Calcutta and I spent the night with Margaret List Jaffie and her family. We surely did have a good visit, and of course she sends you her greetings. Her little girl is an exact image of Margaret except that she has brown eyes. She is a very smart little 4 year-old. They have a very comfortable home and like it here, at least her husband really does. Both of them are learning Hindustani and that speaks well for them. Few officials bother to learn the language. Strange that we should meet out here after all these years. I had seen Margaret in Chicago when I was on furlough, but when I met her here I hardly knew her she had gotten so grey. It was good to see someone from home.

Since coming back the month of June was mostly taken up with three Bible camps and that involves a lot of work. Now I am back across the river in our Kurku village. Ruth should join me this week. She stayed behind to see that the painter actually puts on the two coats of paint on the jeep he gets paid for. Everyone is busy seeding out here. This area raises considerable cotton so that goes in first and rice. Rice in this area is sown dry like wheat. In the real rice centers it is sown in water, or paddy fields. Well, I planted a garden too, but all that is up so far are the zinnias and cucumbers. This rain ought to really bring things on.

This place is about to collapse. We hate to put a lot of time and expense on it now when we are leaving next year and not at all sure we will be able to get back. The rats have been so bad that I have to keep a light burning all night. For some reason they seem to love soap and carry it away if it is left out in the open.

There is some kind of creature out under our wood in the cook house. It makes a funny noise like a cat that is coughing. We aren't exactly pleased at having it around, especially when we don't know what it is. Janki bai declares it is a python and is scared to be in there. I'd be scared too, but I don't think snakes make that kind of noise. John says it is a Ghoose, a huge kind of rat that digs enormous holes. Well it could be for the holes are surely there as fast as we fill them up.

There are advantages to a tumble down place; out in our johnny is the most beautiful, intricate spider web you ever saw. If that were an indoor toilet, in the name of good housekeeping I'd have to take it down, but as it is I have admired and enjoyed it for two days. And there is the most ferocious looking prehistoric reptile hanging around; must be about 6 inches long, but with his horny crest and beady eyes he really puts up quite a front. The most remarkable thing about him is that his head and throat get fiery red when he is disturbed.

The people of the village are always glad to have us come back. That is a good sign to us, but mostly it stems on superstition. It is bad luck to have a house stand empty.

John and Kali, the young couple with us, have the sweetest little baby girl. She will be two months old tomorrow. She probably weighs 7 or 8 pounds now and is nice and plump. John has been very sick with malaria for two days. I was beginning to fear he might have typhoid, but at last the fever has broken in response to quinine.

Well, guess I'll see about some supper. I suppose Scott and Ferol are home for vacation so greetings to you all. This time next year I may be back home with you.

Love Beryl

Pamela Girard

Editor's Notes:

Tenzing Norgay, a Nepalese sherpa, and Sir Edmund Hillary, a New Zealander, were the first climbers to reach the summit of Mount Everest on May 29, 1953. Who reached the summit first was a secret both men took to their graves.

Ellichpur, Amravati Dist., Bombay State, India
January 18, 1957

Dear Bernard and Helen,

It was surely good to hear from you. It doesn't seem possible Ferol LaRae is already married. Time does funny things to you when you are far away. Somehow I expect to find things and people much the same as when I left seven years ago, but everything, including me has changed. Thanks so much for your generous gift. It is nice to be remembered.

I wish I could tell you definitely when we will be arriving, but as yet we have nothing really booked – only promises. However we expect to leave here sometime in March so will surely be in Dakota by May. Right now we are on tour – in tents. We are pitched in the shade of a large mango tree. There are four tents in all, two umbrella tents. In the first are, Harun, a young Southern Indian Brahmin Christian with a real testimony, then John and Kali and the baby in the second. In the big tent are four of us women; Yohanna Bai, 67, Janaki, 50 or so, and Ruth and I, 40ish. Then there is a pup tent which we use for bathing purposes. Dogs and crows are our worst enemies. They swipe everything they can.

The weather is really delightful – for once we have no complaints – neither too hot nor too cold.

Sorry to hear your mother has been ill, Helen. Hope she is better by now. Your folks must be close to 80. Did you sell your house in Mohall?

Ruth and I have just been in Calcutta for a week. It's such a contrast for us to go to a large city. People dress so well – well educated – then to come back to this culture and we feel like two different people! Of course that is what happens when we come home *(from the US)* – takes time to adjust.

See you soon,

Love, Beryl

Dharni, Amravati Dist., B.S., India
June 9, 1958

Dear Bernard and Helen,

My Beulah *(North Dakota)* seems a long way away – hardly seems real that I was even there. We reached Bombay May 14th, and got up country on the 17th. The heat was terrific, and of course, we had to get right at our house. I am glad it is all done now, but I fear we over did it in the heat, for now we are simply exhausted. Of course the rains will come soon and cool us off a bit. At least the rain settles the dust. I hate the dirt blowing all the time.

We really had a good trip back, smooth sailing all the way. We had 10 days between ships, so we started sight-seeing in Rome. When I have time I'm going to write a more detailed account. We were three days in Interlaken, Switzerland and took a trip up the Jungfrau. It was lovely and clean, and very cold. We had one day in Venice. That to me was one of the most interesting places. Yes, we visited the glass blower factories too. Simply amazing to see them take the molten glass from the furnace, blow and pinch it into a tiny glass horse in 3 to 5 minutes or make a huge vase or figurine.

Then we went back to Naples. There we visited the Isle of Capri and Pompeii, and climbed Vesuvius. Pompeii was another fascinating place. We didn't have nearly enough time to see it all

Pamela Girard

– besides we were so cold we couldn't stay any longer (now that I am roasting I wonder how I could have been so cold). The streets of Pompeii are all there, restored just as they were when Vesuvius erupted so many years ago. I've got some rather good slides I'll probably send home after awhile.

Right now we are spending a few days at Khamla – the bungalow we use during hot season. The temperature here is in the 90 s, a contrast to Ramakhera's 114 plus (house temperature).

Love, Beryl

Dharni, Amravati Dist., B.S., India
September 8, 1958

Dear Bernard and Helen,

I've had three letters from you since I've written so it's high time I answered. I don't see how you could make a trip clear to the coast (*Seattle*) after major surgery and now do all that work so soon. But then I've always thought you were an unusual woman – this proves it. I'm surely glad to hear there was no cancer found.

You must have enjoyed your visit with Pam and Scott and Blanche and Bob (*Helen's sister and husband*) and family. Yes, I think Pam and Scott are pretty satisfactory too.

We're having another shower – we've had a lot of rain lately. I went to the bazaar last Sunday (round trip 8 miles). No sooner had we reached the market than rain began pelting down – regular downpour. It flooded all the streams so we had to return by a different route – which meant walking a mile on the main road. The road is made out of crushed rock. Every stream was knee deep or even hip deep – simply tearing along; but the crushed rock was the worst – I was barefoot and I thought I'd never get over that mile. The mud from there was knee deep, but everything was better than that rock.

Letters From India

We're working hard on the Kurku language. A young Jewish fellow from New York was out here working on this language for his degree. He was an expert linguist and gave us a lot of help especially on tone, for Kurku is a tonal language – 4 tones – with glottal stops and other equally difficult sounds. I'm recognizing the tone – reproducing it is another matter. Fortunately for translation work the tone is not important (it is for speaking.) But then we run into other snags. We want to stick to the Hindi script but it doesn't quite fit. Especially we have trouble with the Kurku "a" which is in between the Hindi "a" and "aa" in length.

We (Ruth and I) are experimenting on Kurku primers. Two young men are learning to read so fast that I'm hard put to keep ahead of them with reading material. Then we found that primer was too difficult for the women, so I had to do another – this is probably the model we'll stick to. Honestly, it looks so simple once it's done, but I surely swallowed a lot of aspirin in making it up. Kurku verbs are so complicated with suffixes and infixes, etc. that it's difficult to find a simple verb of one or two syllables.

Say did you ever see a bird dance? The other day I saw a little black fellow dancing before his girl friend. He had his wings, tail and top knot spread and he went through several very intricate dances. He was so cute and funny, I couldn't help laughing. Sad to say his lady friend paid no attention what-so-ever.

Love, Beryl

Ramakhera, Amravati Dist., B.S., India
November 27, 1958

Dear Bernard and Helen,

The calendar says it's Thanksgiving Day back home. Last year I was in Beulah with you folks. Anyway though I couldn't be with you again, I've thought of you off and on all day –

probably you have remembered me too. Well it's 9:15 p.m. here so you may be just stuffing the turkey.

Ruth has been gone to Ellichpur for a couple of days so we haven't had any Thanksgiving dinner this year – though I guess every morning we are thankful for the Lord's protection through the night and every evening for His watch and care through the day.

We had a spell of chilly weather for a while when our blankets and flannel pajamas felt good. Then this week it turned hot again and even rained. The river rose today so I'm wondering if Ruth will have trouble getting back. We had crossed with the jeep, only to have all the brake fluid run out leaving us with no brakes. So back to Ellichpur she had to go.

Honestly the Kurkus can be so exasperating sometimes. So many children die of malnutrition – but do you think they will believe that milk would do the child any good? If the child cries, most mothers won't make the child take the pills or medicine. One day a mother tried to get a <u>spoiled</u> boy to take some medicine. He cried and made a fuss so she quit, but she'd paid for the medicine so she fed it to her little girl who was not sick, but who was willing to drink it.

Our neighbor is a medicine man in his own rights. But sometimes he comes to us too. One day I gave him some atabrine for malaria and told him how to take it. He said he always took them all at once – "work faster that way." And before I could stop him he swallowed (without water) the 2 day's supply!!

Another family had a child we were trying to treat for malnutrition. It was really picking up, but not fast enough to suit them, besides they couldn't stand its crying so they started on opium. When they wouldn't listen to our warning, but continued with the opium, there was nothing we could do but withdraw.

Actually the placenta of a donkey is considered the best treatment for malnutrition. It may be cooked and fed to the patient or a small piece dried and worn as a charm.

Better make this my Christmas letter. May this be a blessed time for you. No more room.

Love, Beryl

Dharni, Amravati Dist., B.S., India
March 10, 1959

Dear Bernard and Helen,

Your air letter announcing your first grandchild arrived Christmas day. That was a nice time for good news from home. Now I'm anxiously awaiting a report of your visit and description of Bret Thomas (I prefer Tommy too.) Your Christmas letter you mentioned still hasn't arrived. I suppose you sent it surface mail – huh?

We've just finished up a 10-day reading campaign in a jungle village. Too bad you couldn't have dropped in for a visit. I think you would have found it interesting as well as exciting. The village is high on a hill in the teak forest. The undergrowth of the jungle came up to one side of our tent. The village well is far below in the valley. Every drop of water is hauled up on someone's head – usually the women's. As a result it is too precious for bathing. That really is a dirty crowd. Ruth and I carried our clothes down to the well and scrubbed them on a rock which works just like a scrub board. By the time we'd puffed our way up the hill, we could sympathize with the villagers.

One morning as we went down, the monkeys suddenly began to hoot and then a barking deer started to bark. Our path was lined by thick undergrowth. We knew there was a tiger around – we were glad to reach the well and the open space. Two days later the tiger killed one of the villager's bullocks not more than a furlong from our tent in those same bushes. The villagers finally tied the dead bullock down – the tiger had moved it once before they got around to tying it – built a platform in a tree and called in a hunter. The tiger was too wary to return. Good thing for if the hunter had only wounded the beast it would then have become a menace to the whole countryside. One gun I saw was an old muzzle loader with the hammer tied up with string. Too bad you weren't around Bernard.

Our reading campaign was successful. Five young men actually finished the primers and can now read well enough to help the others. This was a real test of our new Kurku primers, even in an area where the dialect is a bit different. We found only one word that needs changing in order to be understood in both areas.

But, oh it was hard work! I guess the noise got us, everyone reads as loud as he can and we must out shout them to be heard. Then sitting cross-legged on the ground all day made us so stiff and our knees so sore we could hardly wait until we could crawl into bed at night and stretch out our legs. Still we now have left those fellows reading simple Bible stories. I'm now working on a simple "Life of Christ" in Kurku. I'd hoped to have it done by now but it's not.

Love, Beryl

Editor's Notes:

Helen loved to name every baby born in the family or in Bernard's medical practice. Families usually chose other names much to her chagrin.

Bernard was a champion trapshooter and hunted most of his life..

Ramakhera, Amravati Dist., B.S., India
July 4, 1959

Dear Bernard and Helen,

Fourth of July and I bet a nickel you went fishing!! Right at this point I think a picnic would be nice. It's been so hot here today that the old Missouri *(River)* would be a nice place to go.

We've had only a couple of rains and the heat continues. The nights are too hot for sleep so we start the day exhausted.

(July 5th) We had rain last night and today so we are cool again. And the garden is really growing before our eyes. The temperature has dropped to 80 and we almost need a <u>sweater</u>!

Your airmail letter came to me while we were in Mussoorie. Surely was good to hear from you. I am anxious to see a picture of your grandchild. (According to Indian customs I am also a grandmother as Bernard's oldest sister!) I never did get the Christmas letter you said you sent – so I wonder if I've missed any other mail.

Now we are busy on Kurku translation again. I am working on the Hindi to Kurku dictionary also. I did the Kurku to Hindi dictionary while we were on hot-season leave. It's fascinating work, and I hate to lay it aside – but it does take hours of work. Up to this time I've used file cards building up a lexicon; that is clumsy to carry around – but now in book form I can put my fingers on the word I want in a hurry. Wish all the words would stay in my head!!

We had some tracts and the primer printed up in Mussoorie while we were there. Now a simple reader is the next must and I'm revising the one we were using. The days are too short, but honestly they've been so hot that they seem too long.

I hope you've had rain in Dakota. Pink wrote that they'd had one after a long dry spell. They surely need a crop after so many years of nothing.

We have had a terrible invasion of rats. Finally in desperation we resorted to poison. We never saw rats take the stuff in daylight before. Fortunately 4 of 5 we saw dying before they got into a hole. One got into our wood pile, but Bapuroa found him. We fear one has died in the wall or roof. So we'll smell dead rat for a long time.

A saucy, bold crow has really been a pest. We kept the few eggs we had out back trying to keep them cool with a wet cloth around them. I figured some were disappearing. Finally I caught the crow swiping one. I removed the eggs, but the crow is still sure they must be in something and opens everything. Then he sits on the roof and scolds us in a most raucous voice. He's a mess!

Love, Beryl

Dharni, Amravati Dist., B.S., India
August 11, 1959

Dear Bernard and Helen,

I am sitting in a literature conference of missionaries and nationals from all over India. The discussion right now has more to do with those involved in publishing. There are at least 10 of the major language areas of India represented here. This ought to be a good time to write to you.

This morning's session was valuable. The stress is the necessity of training national Christians for creative writing, and of the need for better and more attractive reading material. Tomorrow the discussion will be more along the distribution lines. I am more interested in that, and of course the actual preparation of material. I'm anxious to try to help some of our young people get established in a Christian bookshop where they might become self-supporting and yet get the Christian literature out.

It was good to hear from you last week. In fact I received a letter from Merle and Gen the same day so I really felt like I'd had a visit with you all. Good thing birthdays and Christmas come around once a year!! I do think poor little Tommy *(Bret Thomas)* is going to suffer from those horrible names. Don't they take any pictures of him?

No, I never did receive your Christmas letter so if there was a check in it, you'd better stop payment. Lots of mail is lost. I believe air mail is safer than sea mail. From this end much of our air mail is lost for the temptation to remove the expensive stamps is too much for some clerks. We try to see every air mail stamp cancelled; but sometimes this isn't possible.

We've had rain day and night for over 3 weeks. We are thankful for the coolness, but the crops are being damaged by so much rain. Usually we have rain a day or two at a time then a break then more rain. Some villages have been washed away by flooding rivers. Our own river is high, and I waded through deep mud all the way out to the mail road. But there was a well by the side of the road and a young Kurku kindly drew water for me so that I washed off the thick mud from my feet, legs and washed the bottom of my sari which soon died in the wind. I was presentable when the bus finally came along.

Life is certainly not as complicated over here as it is at home in the States. Language work takes all my time. It is fascinating work, and I'm usually still at it up to 10 p.m. Slowly but surely the language problems clear up.

Last week a man was bitten by a snake. Since he was bitten in the jungle, that is, outside of the house, he was not permitted to enter. (If he should be bitten in the house he could not go out – bad luck to go through a door.) He was lying out in the open with all the medicine men chanting and blowing and shouting. All night long this continued and he lived. It was evidently a poisonous snake, but not all are deadly to man and the medicine men got all the credit. But they never lose face. If the victim dies, they assure the people it was his fate, no one could save him if it were his fate to die from a snake.

No woman is permitted near a snake bit victim so although we have anti-venom serum no one dares call us. Only one young man has ever come for treatment. Fortunately he came at once and we treated him. He lived though we feel sure he was bitten by a viper.

Write again. I'm always eager to hear.

Love, Beryl

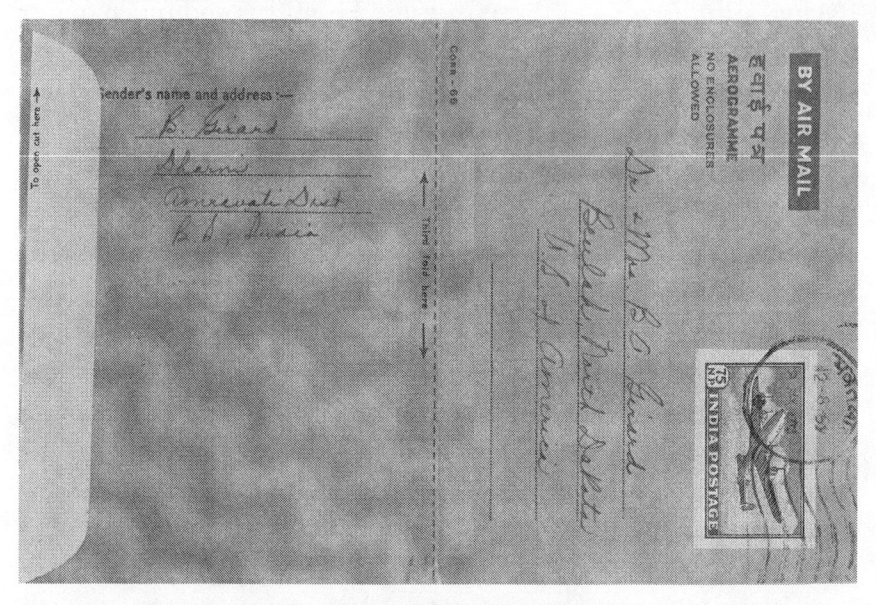

Ramakhera, Deratalai, Nimare Dist., M.P. India
January 19, 1963

Dear Bernard and Helen,

I actually received your Christmas letter on Christmas eve, but we had such a crowd here and were so busy, I didn't get to open it until the next day, and then hardly did more than look at the pictures. Thanks much for the check too. I was so pleased with the picture of you and the grandchildren. And the one of Bernard with the trophy *(shooting)* was so natural – made me homesick for you all.

I'm surely looking forward to seeing you – only trouble is trying to find time to visit everyone. Since I'll be in school all summer, June through August and then in Minneapolis or St. Paul for more school (and deputation) September through December. That really takes a lot of my time.

Last week I was at a huge Hindu fair. We camped in the midst of the bullock selling place. Before pitching our tents the fellows scraped aside rich, rich fertilizer that I coveted for our garden. Well, I ate a good share of it before we got out of there!! Wind blew it back into our food, eyes, hair. But we had a good time. People bought our books and listened to the Gospel day after day.

This week I've worked day and night on Mark. I still have four chapters to translate before April. Some of the portions left are difficult too. Next week, the 30th, I am taking our trunks to Bombay to be sent off. Ruth and I are flying as far as England, stopping to see the Holy Land enroute so our baggage has to be sent ahead.

I'll bring you a piece of raw silk. It's hard to choose for someone else because there are so many colors and types. If I have enough money, I'll stick in an extra piece so you can take your choice. I have a piece for Pinkie and want to get one for Gen too. I wasn't sure you'd like it, so thought I'd better ask. I can't get any more once my trunk is gone – no reason to carry it by air.

We are due into New York April 29th. It'll take a week I suppose in Chicago to get doctor's clearance then I'll head for North Dakota.

Love, Beryl

Editor's Note:

Beryl always came home loaded with wonderful gifts – teak elephant bookends and candleholders, carpets, saris, raw silk, silver jewelry, and books and toys for the children. Recently I was talking to my younger son about Aunt Beryl. He asked, "Do you remember those transparent leaves that she sent to us when we were little?" He was fascinated by the intricate pictures painted on them of elephants and tigers.

Dharni, Amravati Dist., B.S., India
March 7, 1963

Dear Bernard and Helen,

These last days are so busy they leave us exhausted. But I've finished the translation of Mark and have copied - and copied – and finally got it all hectographed for checking purposes in different areas for differences in dialect. Well, now we are applying for permits to leave. Takes more permits to leave then to enter India!!

This will be a busy furlough for I will be spending so much time in study. But I'm surely hoping to drop in often at your place. Usually we have 2 months rest period when we first return, but I will have to forfeit one month in order to attend a translator's workshop in Mexico. But there is another month before we return and all the holidays. Do you remember Frost's poem, "The Woods"? – The last lines go:

> "The woods are lovely, dark and deep,
> But I have promises to keep,
> And miles to go before I sleep,
> And miles to go before I sleep."
>
> **(Robert Frost)**

Ruth and I leave here on the 3rd and leave Bombay April 8th. Maybe I've written that before. Ruth isn't well. Probably complete fatigue, on top of or because of amoeba and filariasis. We have three other missionaries seriously ill right now too.

I will write you when I arrive in New York.

Love, Beryl

Editor's Note:

Filariasis (or elephantiasis) is an infection, spread by mosquitoes from person to person, where small thread-like parasitic worms live in the human lymph system. They restrict the flow of lymph fluid which causes swelling, scarring and infections.

Bombay, India
April 8, 1963

Dear Bernard and Helen,

I've been remembering you both have birthdays in April. May the Lord bless and give you a happy year.

We leave Bombay tonight at midnight. We go directly to Cairo and from there to Jerusalem. We'll be there by 9 in the morning tomorrow. We have about 7 days there, and from there we are flying directly to New York arriving in New York on the 17th.

Ruth isn't well, and in no condition to be running around so after the Holy Land we are coming directly home. I'm glad to be getting home earlier myself. We'll be in Chicago until we are through with the doctor and all the tests he requires. Filariasis may be Ruth's whole trouble – but it may be something else. I'm frankly concerned. I don't think I'll have anything worse than amoeba.

We had such a time getting our permits to return that we were simply exhausted by the time we reached Bombay. I've gotten rested up, but Ruth doesn't pick up. We will see what we can in Jordan – but it will have to be at a leisurely pace.

I must rest a bit before we leave.

Lots of love, Beryl

Apartado 13, Ixmiquilpan, Hidalgo, Mexico *(Language School)*
July 20, 1963

Dear Helen and Bernard,

Your lovely card and letter and gift arrived right on my birthday. Thanks so much. I won't cash the check until I return to the States so it won't show up on your bank report, statement I guess it is called, until then.

Well, I was surprised that Bernard had all that surgery. Had he been having trouble with that heel for a long time?

Yes, the TWA check was sent down here. I guess it was forwarded from Williston. I had put down the cost of everything as it would be for replacing here in the States, so the check does cover everything. Of course there were some things that I have picked up in different lands that could not be replaced here. Oh, well, I have long ago learned not to put my affections on <u>things</u>. *(Some of her belongings were lost in transit from India).*

I have been so busy here that I have not felt like going any place on the weekends to sight-see. I have had my fill of that anyway. However, last weekend I did go to visit some friends. The bus trip took us on beyond Mexico City to Pueblo. The pass over the mountains was over 10,000 feet and than in the distance were two snowcapped volcanoes. They were beautiful in the early morning (over 16,000 feet.) I also heard a serenade. A store had a sale on and had hired these fellows to play and sing out front to draw the crowd. They were all dressed in Spanish costume and the singer had one of these huge sombreros on. Oh, they were really elegant. The girls I was with had a hard time getting me to move on.

This workshop is proving most helpful to me. I have finished checking the Gospel of Mark with the consultants, but there are still a lot of hard passages that I am working on. The lectures reveal something new each time. I guess it is good to be on the ignorant side. That way it is so much fun when you learn something new. It must be boring to know everything. Some of the hardest parts of the Scriptures to translate into another language are figures of speech. If they are translated literally there is absolutely no meaning to them. The lectures on how to transfer the meaning into another language is not only helpful, but interesting.

The workshop closes here on August 31st. Then I have to be in Winona Lake, Indiana on September 9th so I guess the Custer drama is out as far as I am concerned. Ruth may drive down here to get me and then we will go together to Winona Lake. Otherwise I will take a bus to St. Paul, leave my baggage there and then go on to Winona Lake.

Yes, I can imagine the gun talk that went on when Merle *(Beryl's brother)* was there. Do you two try to out-trade each other? That would be interesting to see and hear.

The woman I live with made me a birthday cake yesterday. In fact I had already had one on the 7th, with two other missionaries who had birthdays at the same time. So I really had two cakes this year. Well, all this cake doesn't seem to make me fat. I guess I must be feeding too many amoebas. I have taken a course of entro-viaform since coming here, but I guess that is too mild.

The fruit down here is delicious and there are plenty of vegetables available in the market. In fact the market is very much like an Indian market. One difference – someone is always dragging a pig through to sell, and there is pork cooking all over the place. No more news.

   Love, Beryl

Ramakhera, Deratalai, Nimar Dist, M.P. India
June 27, 1964

Dear Bernard and Helen,

   Well, I can hardly wait to hear of your trip East, of the graduation, and of the new grandson. Then I suppose you have gone to Williston *(North Dakota)* and to Colorado, too.
   We got into Bombay May 26th. The harbor was full of ships waiting to pull into dock to unload, so our ship had to drop anchor in the bay and wait her turn. We got off in a launch and got our cabin baggage off, but the hold baggage we could not get until the ship docked. Then everything closed for three days when Nehru died. He was a great man and dearly loved here in India, so naturally there would be a period of mourning. Well, that delayed things so that we had to wait 14 days in Bombay. I guess it was all for the best, for it was terribly hot in Ramakhera and there in Bombay I went swimming once or twice a day while we waited.
   It was very hot here when I first moved in. Ruth did not even attempt to stay here as she simply can not stand the heat. But then we began to get showers every night and this week we have had so much rain that the weather has been very comfortable. It will be hot and steamy when the sun comes out again. But part of our garden is already up. Ruth will come out at the end of July probably.
   It was good to see everyone in our village, and they seem glad that we are back. A year away from the language always leaves us rusty and so I am working hard now on both Hindi and Kurku. The feminine and masculine endings in Hindi always give us

trouble when we get away from it for a while. I have no trouble in comprehending what I hear, but I find myself searching for words that have escaped me when I talk. It will take about a month to get back to where I was when I went home.

The police were here in the village today. Someone beat a cow so badly that it died. One of the children claims to have seen who did it, but the fellow denies it. Actually this case will drag on for months even years. The fellow could be given a jail sentence for killing a cow. Sad part of it is that the fellow accused of beating the cow has plenty, while the people who owned the cow are desperately poor and had just gotten the cow not too long ago, a heifer. I saw it just after it had been beaten and didn't think it could live.

We had smooth sailing coming over. There was only one day that the swells made the ship roll quite a bit. We stopped at Ceuta, Alexandria, Karachi, and then Bombay. In Alexandria we pulled in just a few hours after Kruschev and his party had arrived. We were docked just across from his ship, but of course did not see him. We had time to make the trip to Cairo. I had made this trip some years ago; what really interested me was the great change in the country since their independence *(from British rule)*. What was then desert is now irrigated and fertile land. The wheat fields were as beautiful as those of North Dakota, although on a smaller scale. Oh, yes, I saw a whale this trip. I had seen them spouting before, but this time I saw it surface through some glasses we had borrowed.

We brought a couple kittens out here to keep the rats down. The way they tear around is almost as bad as the rats. However, I like cats and HATE rats. These kittens insist on being in my lap as soon as I sit down, and when I am standing they are under my long sari. And as they are either fighting or sleeping all the time they do get to be pests. Still they are fun to watch.

Love, Beryl

Pamela Girard

Editor's Notes:

B. A. and Helen traveled to Philadelphia for their son Scott's graduation from medical school (Temple) and meet their new grandson.

Nehru became India's first Prime Minister in August 1947. After Gandhi's assassination on January 30, 1948, he became India's most powerful political leader. Nehru was instrumental in helping and revising Lord Mountbatten's plan for Independence from the British Empire. He also was in power during riots and armed conflict with Pakistan over Kashmir and a border conflict between China and India after China invaded Tibet. These disputes had a devastating personal impact on Nehru and his health rapidly declined. After his death, he was succeeded by his daughter, Indira Gandhi. She was assassinated in 1984, after serving as prime minister for 15 years.

Ramakhera, Deratalai, Nimar Dist, M.P. India
December 27, 1964

Dear Bernard and Helen,

Your letter came the day before Christmas. The picture is good, and the letter full of news and well written. I think you better start writing a book in your spare time, though I am not sure whether the title would be "North Dakota – General Practitioner" or "North Dakota – Hunting and Fishing." Thanks for the gift. I will save it for a good vacation sometime.

Well, our Christmas celebrations are nearly over. I was very tired yesterday after a week of preparation and then two days of guests. Ruth brought in a group from the area where she is working and with the folks here we were 51 for supper. The men did the cooking and serving, but ran out of rice and had to cook some more. The Kurkus are tremendous eaters when they can get food. 2 ½ cups of uncooked rice their measure for one serving. Then we had slides and a good sing afterwards. To me the highlight of the whole thing was that two of the men of our group here in Ramakhera and Situ bai, the woman of whom I write so often, made up new Kurku songs for the occasion. This is the first time I have been able to get them to do this, and they are all good.

Tonight I must go to a dinner in Dharni. This lady is a very good cook so it ought to be worth the four-mile hike to get it. I will have to stay overnight and then another four miles back. Good thing these festivals come only once a year. I must be getting old (don't hear anyone calling me kid anymore).

Ruth was here over night and then had to return with the group that she had brought. This is a very busy season for farmers for the millet crop is ripe and no one dares leave their fields. There is a lot of stealing going on for prices are so high, that many cannot afford to purchase grain.

Bapuroa and his family are still here. They will leave after New Year's. The house will be very quiet when they are gone. I have to leave for a couple of weeks in January and Ruth will be staying here until I return. I guess she will be glad the kids are gone as she doesn't like the racket.

It is still only 60 in here and my fingers are so stiff I can't hit the right keys. The sun is getting up now though so that it will soon warm us. We sit out in the sun for our morning worship service (this is Sunday.)

It is a shame not to fill up this whole air form, but I must close here. I wanted to let you know right away that I received your letter with the check in it.

Love, Beryl

Pamela Girard

Ramakhera, Deratalai, Nimar Dist, M.P. India
April 3, 1966

Dear Helen and Bernard,

    Our day is just beginning and it promises to be a hot one. Each day the temp climbs a bit higher. Yesterday it hit 105 in our room. As far as I can determine once the temperature is over 100 a few more degrees more or less doesn't make too much difference, although of course it is some satisfaction to note how high the temp goes. I do not mind the heat as long as I keep occupied; though it does make me sleepy and it is the period between 12 and 2 p.m. when I am too sleepy to do anything and still wake up feeling like pancake with the heat pressing down on me that is the hardest. Ruth's fan is here and I will bring back the battery next time I go to Ellichpur and see if I can use it. I usually end up with hay fever when I sleep under a fan. The nights are still delightful (outside of course, it would be impossible to sleep inside).
    Yesterday I watched one of the wicked hot season whirlwinds dancing over the roof tops of the village. It removed several of the grass roofs so that the air was swirling with huge teak wood leaves as though thousands of vultures were circling over head. Then it turned down the lane and scooped up all the fine grey dust so that it looked like a huge pillar of smoke from a mighty fire. No wonder the Kurkus call this an evil spirit. My house is full of fine dust, hair, eyes, everything. Still dry as it is the trees are bringing out their new leaves; some come out bright brown, red, different shades of green, yellow. All turn green eventually. Everyone hopes the rains will come early for the rivers and wells are all nearly dry. Yesterday the water the boy brought from our well was thick mud. He said he would try another well, and came back with clear water. I was pleased. Then he informed me that a cow had fallen into the well and no one else in the village was using that water. I gulped, but sent him for more. Assuredly it must have been a holy cow.

Last week I camped under some mango trees in a distant village. There, an illiterate Christian couple, are giving such an effective witness, that several Kurkus now believe in the Lord. I went there to teach them. We must go back again. But I don't know when I can find the time. I ran into something new there that I could very easily do without. Usually we consider tea a safe drink, but here I was offered 'sherbut'. It is made of river water (no wells in the village) and sweetened with sugar. Oh, well, I can always take another course of amoeba treatment.

Tomorrow I must leave again to go to the wedding of Janki bai's son. You may remember her name for she used to live with us. Then on the 16th of this month Hiru will be married. Here the groom provides the wedding clothes for the bride and the bride's parents buy the groom's wedding clothes. In this case Hiru has been under my care since she was tiny, and so I have had to pay for the suit for the groom. Weddings cost quite a bit even though one tries to keep them simple. Still the clothes will be their best dress for several years and so it is rather an investment I guess.

Bapuroa and Juli went to Ellichpur yesterday so that Juli could see the doctor before he goes away for the hot season. Hiru and I kept their second boy, Jarji (George) with us. He is an awfully cute little kid – five years old. It is the first time he has stayed away from his parents, but he has only cried a little at bed time.

I've had no more news concerning Ruth for more than a week – but that was encouraging. The doctor now believes Ruth will recover *(from a severe stroke)* though it will take time. She has to learn many things all over again. At times she seems to remember, then again is confused. It's confusing even to a well person to be suddenly transplanted from one culture to another. The mailman should have come today. Guess it's too hot for him too.

Wish you could see my beautiful moss roses. It's amazing to see them so beautiful in all this heat. Everything else dies. But I've discovered petunias can also stand the heat – have them in pots. A few flowers help the morale, and I save all my water for them.

Love, Beryl

Pamela Girard

Editor's Note:

Once when she was writing letters in 120° heat, cobras began entering the little house for shade. She killed them all. In fact in the time she was there she killed more than the village medicine man.

There are more details about Ruth's condition in the letter to Shirley and Al, dated March 19, 1966.

Chapter 3
Letters to Minnesota

*"I was struck by the missionaries' spirit
of thankfulness despite deplorable conditions."
(Eloise Merrill)*

After traveling with a guide by foot and raft to find Beryl

Dharni, Amroati Dist., M.P., India
February 18, 1954

Dear Shirley and Allen,

Thanks for all the snapshots and your good letter. Tony is a cute little rascal. His granddad sent some slides too. I've not seen them projected yet and I'm anxious to see them on a screen. Yes, I like to get good pictures of my family.

I'm glad you are so happy in your little home *(St. Paul, Minnesota)* and that you are seeking to establish a Christian home. Jesus Christ is a living Savior and the Bible is the Word of God. It should be read daily, for it is our spiritual food.

I don't know the hospital your pastor referred to. India is a very large country – I'd probably know where it is if he mentioned the name of the town or village where it is located.

Our hot season has already begun and oh, how hot it already is. This promises to be a very severe season.

We are having a small conference here in our village. There are some 20 Christians here. There is only one shade tree in the village and it is the garden of our "enemy" the medicine man. He said that we could put up our tents there however. He was drunk the day we began when he found out we didn't have the "radio" (loud-speaking system.) He was so mad that he ordered us all out. Mr. Grubbs pacified him by going in to Dharni to get his P.A. system.

We've had big crowds out to hear the Gospel each night, but they surely don't sit quietly. Without Christ they have no hope and yet they are so afraid of evil spirits that they are afraid to leave the old ways.

We laughed the other day to hear that one family had named their son, "The Riches of Manure." He is called "Manure" for short. Their first son died and neighbors advised them to give this child a bad name so that the evil spirits wouldn't take him also. They live in constant fear of evil spirits.

We are going to have fish curry for supper, head and all. Guess Allen didn't like the Indian food I cooked when I was home so there's no use inviting you for dinner. It's pretty hot with chili peppers and spices, but I'm so used to it that I don't notice how hot it is anymore.

No, we do not have snow here – not even frost - and from February through July we roast. August and September are also hot, but the rains cool things off a bit.

Love, Beryl

Letters From India

Editor's Notes:

Al is Merle's son and Beryl's and Bernard's nephew. Al's wife Shirley and Beryl were prayer partners.
On one trip home Beryl cooked an Indian meal for us. Even cutting the spices in half left us teary-eyed and unable to speak.

Dharni, Amrosti District, M.P., India
June 30, 1954

Dear Shirley, Allen and Tony,

Bout time I answered your March 30th letter. It is always good to hear from you. Tony must be quite a young man now. Hope you got enough money saved up for your vacation.

This is supposed to be our rainy season. We had two good rains in the middle of June, then after that terrific heat. Our little Indian hut gets almost unbearable and we're wondering how much more we could stand. But our Lord knows what we need and yesterday and last night we had a good rain. Today it is steamy but cooler.

We have a garden, corn, pumpkin, cucumbers and tomato. The beans and carrots we planted haven't come up yet and I doubt they will now. The only vegetable we can buy is onion so we are anxious to have a good garden. We can get some greens from the jungle so that helps. Really they are just weeds, but they taste good.

We now have two cats and though they would be scared of a rat if they did see one. I guess the rats must be just as scared of them, for we haven't had a rat in the house since we came back. One of the kittens is a jungly cat, grey with black stripes. She is very timid and doesn't like to be petted, but on the other hand, she can't bear to be left alone and is always wherever Ruth and I are. The other is a reddish yellow with bright blue eyes, very soft and lovable. He is so funny that we have had a lot of good laughs over some of his antics. But best of all we appreciate not having rats run over us at night as soon as the lights go out as they did before.

The farmers here are busy sowing their fields. They use a wooden plow and bullocks pull it. The women come behind planting everything by hand. Most everyone in this area is sowing cotton this year. Later in March they will be able to raise wheat. This is not rice area, but they plant some.

It is good to see the countryside getting green again. Our well is nearly dry and the water we get out of it is nearly black. Once the rains really set in, the well will fill up again. A girl fell in the other day. How she escaped without some broken bones I don't know for the well is deep with rock jutting out on the sides and very little water in the bottom to break her fall. Everyone came running to give advice, but it was a long time before anyone actually did anything about getting her out. Finally the men lowered a small cot into the well and the girl climbed onto it and so was pulled out.

That same morning we were called out to see a huge snake. It was harmless and everyone insisted that it brought good luck, for instance, if it were in their grain bin, the grain would never run out. For some time I have heard the Korkus talking about this snake. It is supposed to have a head on each end, but look as I could, I saw only one head. It is true it had no tail as snakes usually do and both head and the end of its body are perfectly round. Still all insisted that for one month it travels forward with one head and then next month goes the other way with the other head.

Good to hear that you and Allen take such an interest in your church. The Bible teaches that every Christian is to be a witness, that is, that everyone who believes in Jesus Christ should try to make Him known to others. You know there is a great difference in knowing about a person and knowing a person. There is a great difference in knowing about Jesus Christ and knowing Him as your personal Savior from sin. The Bible teaches that if any one be in Christ then he is a new person, old desires and old ways of living will pass away and he will want to do the things that please the Lord. The Bible teaches that if we love Jesus Christ, then should keep his commandments. Read your Bible daily and have family devotions together, the Lord will bless your home if you put Him first in all things.

Haven't heard from any of my family for ages it seems. Even Pinkie who always writes so faithfully hasn't written for over a month. I wonder if she is sick. Probably just awfully busy with her five children and garden.

We can no longer use a jeep on this side of the river so every place we go, we travel on foot. Last weekend I did 18 miles and in this heat, I really felt it.

Tony would like the cuckoo bird that calls during the rainy season. The children here call back at him coo-coo and he will answer indefinitely – usually the kids get tired of the game before the bird does. This is the only season of the year that he calls.

Write when you have time. I am always glad to hear from you. God bless you, all three.

Love, Beryl

Editor's Note:

There was no refrigeration so it took a great deal of thought and preparation to manage her food in such a hot climate. She gardened for fresh vegetables but had to buy other food every day. Of course this entailed another long walk. She once told Al that she felt like she was in paradise when she visited here. There was running water that could actually run hot, indoor plumbing, air conditioning and miracle of miracles, refrigerators.

Pamela Girard

Dharni, Amroati Dist., M.P., India
February 16, 1955

Dear Shirley, Allen and Tony,

    I was waiting to hear about the new baby. Glad to hear all went well and that Cindy Lee is fat and healthy. I guess Tony is really excited these days – huh?

    I am camped under a very tall and not too shady tree. These days are spent in touring from village to village. Our house is a tent, our bed the ground, and our stove a camp fire. A fellow came through the village with fish today so we are having fish curry tonight – smells good already.

    Our hot season is beginning and we really feel the heat in the tents. We are busy going from house to house all day and a big meeting at night where we sing, witness. We preach the Gospel – telling the old, old story that is still new to these folks that Jesus Christ came into the world to save sinners, died on the cross, rose again and lives to save anyone who will believe on Him. With me are two young fellows about like Allen and an older man who is our evangelist, also a dear old lady who has been with us for years.

    February 22nd. This is as far as I got, then was too busy to finish this. Now I'm back in our house and Ruth has gone out on tour. It has already gotten very hot - 98 in our house today and it only the beginning of the hot season. Guess we'll just plain melt before it cools off again in August. Even our cats are seeking cool spots these days. I've been trying to do some language study – but the heat makes me sleepy and I've not accomplished much.

    It is wheat harvest time over here now. Each stalk of grain is pulled up by the roots and tied into a big bundle. 11 bundles go to the owner of the field; the 12th bundle goes to the laborer. Everyone in the village is gone from very early morning to noon or so. Anyone who wants to work can – no need to ask before hand. The children like to roast the wheat heads and eat them that way. The rest of the wheat is thoroughly dried in the sun, and then stored in the earthen grain bins until some festival or wedding; then it is ground into flour in their stone hand mills.

For the Korkus wheat is for special occasions. Their daily bread is made from jawar, a type of Kaffir corn. It is good, but we find it rather heavy, and won't eat it more than once a day so we have wheat and rice at the other two meals. When we have time we bake up some of our own bread – but there is no time for cooking these days – we eat Indian food with our Indian family.

There isn't anything I need right now, but later if I need something I'll let you know. Course I'd like a picture of you all now and then.

Love, Beryl

Pamela Girard

Top: Beryl teaching her first reading class.
Middle: Washing clothes.
Bottom Left: Beryl and Sukhalal.
Bottom Right: Inspecting her garden.

Ramakhera, Dertalai, Nimar District, M.P India
December 17, 1955

Dear Allen, Shirley, Tony and Cindy Lee,

Looks like this will be late for Christmas greetings, but anyway you will know I was thinking of you. Trust this will be a very happy time for you all and the Lord Jesus whose birthday we commemorate may be real and precious to you. He came as a babe in Bethlehem for only one reason – to redeem us all from our sin. His work was complete when he died and rose again – now it is up to us to accept His sacrifice by faith – that is believing in Him and living according to His Word. How we ought to love Him for his love towards us.

I've missed your letters, Shirley. Guess you are kept busy with your two babies – huh? Hope I'll have some pictures of you all now at Christmas time.

We've been living in tents the past two weeks as we tour new villages. The tents get awfully hot in the day time for the temperature is in the 80's then, and at night those tents are like an icebox for the temperature drops into the 50's and a very heavy dew soaks everything. Our little mud house seems like a palace when we return to chairs and a table and beds.

This year we are trying to go to villages where we have never been before. Some are afraid of us – especially the women and children, but they are curious too and so crowd around to hear what we have to say. Some come for medicine. One lady wanted medicine to protect her from evil spirits when she works in the jungle. Ruth told her that medicine doesn't come in bottles, but that Jesus Christ could protect her if she would believe in Him.

All Korkus fear evil spirits. If someone gets sick they think it is either evil spirits or that someone has cursed them. So they call the medicine man that ties some charm on them and chants some incantations to counteract the evil spirits. How thankful we should be that we do not live in this awful fear – yet without Christ there is no peace or hope.

Pamela Girard

Do write when you can. I enjoy hearing about your little family. Where does Allen work? Tell me all the news. God bless and keep you.

Love, Beryl

Ramakhera, Deratalai, Nimar Dist., M.P.
September 22, 1960

Dear Shirl, Al, Tony and Cindy,

Your two letters came ages ago. All my time goes into language work so I really neglect my family and friends. But I do think of you often and appreciate your letters and pictures. Tony and Cindy are really growing up fast.

I just had my supper. I'm here alone – that is Ruth is gone. Astar Bai the old lady who lives with us is here and so are Bapurao and Juli and their baby, Jrel. He's a fat little brown rascal – awfully cute and we love him dearly. Oh, I started to tell you I had waffles for supper. I have an old fashioned waffle iron that works on an oil stove.

What a time you had with that needle in your foot. It must have been very painful. I've been hobbling lately too. I stubbed my foot against the door 2 weeks ago. I guess I broke the fourth toe on my right foot. Well, the swelling had gone down, in fact I'd hiked 8 miles, then if I didn't run into a chair and bang the same toe again. Now it's all swollen. I should either live in a house without furniture else wear shoes.

Glad to hear you are enjoying the adult Sunday school class. The Bible has the answer to our problems. Salvation is a personal thing. You have to decide for yourself either to accept Christ or reject Him. No middle ground. I wish I were closer so I could show you verses from the Bible myself, but even when I was home *(on furlough)* I didn't really get over to your house for a visit did I? Next time will be different I hope.

We have two cats to keep the rats down and actually there isn't a rat around - wonderful peace. But the cats are so crazy. One is the regular village cat – all light grey with black stripes. It looks tigerish. The other is white with grey splotches and a grey tail. The village kids are amazed – think he looks like a rabbit – so that's his name, "The Rabbit." Does he ever scold if we leave him alone.

Pamela Girard

We've had no rain all September and everything is drying up – and of course with no rain the days are terribly hot again. There are a few clouds over head tonight. Hope it rains. I have to hike out tomorrow (four miles) to get a bus to Ellichpur. But I don't even mind hiking in the mud if we'd just get some rain.

Love to all, Beryl

Editor's Notes:

Beryl went barefoot most of the time and found it the best way to travel through the mud during the wet season. It was very hard to adjust to wearing shoes when she was on furlough. It was also hard to adjust to the unbelievable abundance we had in the US and how we took it all for granted.

Ramakhera, Deratalai, Nimar Dist., M.P.
January 19, 1963

Dear Shirley, Al, Tony and Cindy,

I was so happy to receive your letter. I was glad for the pictures. Tony and Cindy are so grown up, and Al looks so much like his Dad used to. But most of all I rejoice over the good news your letter brought, Shirley, that you and Tony too, are trusting in the Lord for your salvation.

Now Allen, how about you? I think of you all so often and have prayed so often that all of my own family might know the Savior who has changed my own life and given it real meaning.

I hope this time (while on furlough) we can have more time together – though I know I'll be about run ragged with school and speaking engagements. Jesus gives a new and fuller life. "Therefore if any man be in Christ he is a new creature – old things have passed away, behold all things are become new." II

Cor: 5.21. I didn't always believe that – but the day I decided to live completely for the Lord everything changed.

Ruth and I are leaving here in April – we're due in New York April 29th. It will take me a while in Chicago to get through all the doctor's check-ups before I can come on. However, since I will be in St. Paul and Minneapolis from Sept. – Dec. or Jan, I'll stop only briefly in May and go on to Pinkie's. You'd laugh to hear Ruth and me discussing furlough. My hair is straight as a string and hangs to my waist. That's the style here (worn in a pug). Guess maybe I'll have it cut in Bombay before I leave.

The hardest part for both of us is wearing shoes. We wear only sandals – just a strap between the toes and half the time we are barefoot as we don't wear our shoes in the house. In fact I can never find my shoes.

Next week I am taking our trunks to Bombay to be shipped ahead. We are traveling part way by air – stopping off to see the Holy Land – so our trunks have to go on ahead. I wouldn't be surprised but that Tony and Cindy will find something they'll like in that trunk. There are so many children now that I need an awfully big trunk. Problem is it's easy to find things girls like – I'm not so sure about the boys.

You must have had a fine Christmas with regular family reunion. Gen has already promised to send pictures.

Lots of love, Beryl

Editor's Notes:

Al, or "Big Al" as he was sometimes called, was and is still a great tease. When he and I were checking some facts about Beryl's life, he told me that she was never quite sure about his faith and his teasing. I told him that I wasn't surprised. Once after Beryl retired, they were sitting in a doctor's waiting room, Beryl told him that it was only fair that he took care of her as she often took care of him when he was a baby. "There's one difference," Al said, "I don't do diapers."

Pamela Girard

Ramakhera, Dertalai, Nimar Dist., M.P.. India
August 31, 1965

Dear Shirl, Al, Tony, Cindy and Glen,

It has been ages since I have written to you and even longer since I have heard from you. I often wonder how you all are. I am sure the children are all busy and growing up fast. It has been well over a year now since I left you there in St. Paul.

This has been a busy year for me. I guess all the years go by like this, but this year marks our 20th anniversary in India. I remember the first thing I noticed in Bombay besides the sticky heat, was the millions of crows. They were everywhere caw, cawing. They still are. Even here in the village, they sit in our trees and scold us.

Now before I go very far, I must tell you that Miss Lilla Kirkpatrick, the missionary who works here with us and is now on furlough, is going to be in St. Paul at the Gladstone Baptist Church on Sept. 7th. That is all the information I have, so why don't you call the church and see what time the meeting is to be and go and hear her. I am sure Gen would like to go. Lilla may have pictures. I have written to her to be sure and try to go and see you, but I don't think she can possibly get my letter. You might not even get this one in time. You may remember that she did come to visit at Merle and Gen's when Tony was a baby. She is a delightful person and you would all enjoy meeting her again. Besides, then she could give me news of you. Be sure to call Gen and tell her. I know she would like to meet her again. Merle too if he is home.

We have had the driest season I have ever known in India. Last week we got our first good rains though and so now everything looks good, though it is all late. My garden is just beginning to bear. Now it is hot and dry again. We will need a lot more rain if there is to be any wheat. That is not planted until late Sept. or Oct. and in the meantime the fields need to soak in moisture. There will be no rain after August. Everywhere the food situation is difficult. Some places nothing is available. Here there is plenty though the prices are very high and that makes it almost unattainable to many.

I must leave tomorrow for a week at another station helping with another translation. I rather hate leaving now the garden is just getting nice. After all when I plant something I like to enjoy the benefits of it. I will have to hike out and then get a bus and then a train and then another train. Until it seems there is no end to the journey; while if I could go cross country, it would only a matter of a few hours.

How are things at your church? Do you all still go every Sunday? I liked your young minister very much. He has a real concern that others should come to know Jesus Christ as their own personal Savior.

I must close and get supper. Perhaps I may think of something else to add later. Greetings to your mother and father, Shirley, and of course to Merle and Gen.

Love, Beryl

Ramakhera, Deratalai, Nimar Dist., M.P., India
September 28, 1965

Dear Shirley, Allen, Tony, Cindy and Glen,

The very day I mailed my last letter to you, I received your letters. I was so pleased to receive such good letters from Tony and Cindy and all the pictures, and of course, Shirley's newsy letter. I think of you all often and miss you. I will be writing to both Tony and Cindy later, but it will go surface mail and will take longer than this one. The pictures were so good. Glen is such a cute little rascal.

Over here we have an uneasy peace. We hardly know what to expect. I've worked day and night getting my dictionary together so I could carry it out in case we have to move. I could not take

Pamela Girard

my files and couldn't bear to think of losing years of work. Now I have the rough draft ready and can now type it up any place.

We have not had nearly enough rain and everything is drying up under a blazing sun. We have lovely tomatoes because we've carried water, but there is danger of the well drying up too, so we can't take too much water.

Glad Tony and Cindy had such good Bible camps. Trust you to get to your retreat, Shirley. The picture of your entire family is so good.

Must close now,

Love, Aunt Beryl

Editor's Note:

The uneasy peace to which Beryl refers was called the "Second Kashmir War" fought between April 1965 and September 1965 between India and Pakistan over the disputed region of Kashmir. The first was fought in 1947. It was generally believed India won, but conflicts continued which eventually led to another war in 1971.

Ramakhera, Deratalai, Nimar Dist., M.P., India
March 19, 1966

Dear Shirl, Al, Tony, Cindy and Glen,

I've been on the go so much since February 1st – hardly more than a week at home. I've had no time to write. I did get a letter off to Gen telling her of Ruth's sickness – the brain hemorrhage. She was flown home for surgery. However, 3 days after surgery there was further bleeding and a set back. It seems this last bleeding caused brain damage. The reports have been very sad, but the last letter a week ago was much more encouraging. Lilla Kirkpatrick has delayed her return to special *(nursing care)* for her, since I can't. I've written a detailed account that you may have received by now.

People all over are praying for her – in fact Lilla wrote that only a miracle of the Lord could restore Ruth now. It is wonderful to know that those days of miracles are not over and the Lord is still able to heal. Do pray for her and share this news with Gen and Merle.

Your parcel was there in Ramakhera when I returned for a couple of days after I came home from Bombay. It was such fun opening it and taking out each item. Eileen Prickett had gone with me so I couldn't be alone right after Ruth left, and she loves liquorices so I share that with her. I like peanut brittle and I've not felt like baking so that has been my dessert these days. Thanks so much for everything. It really came at a time that I needed a lift.

Merle and Gen's parcel came at that time too. I am so glad to have all the dried fruit – and I'll have to make some cookies someday with the butterscotch chips.

I've such a busy program lined up for months – now with Ruth gone I must try to visit the Khamla area too. I still have her books and some things there to sort out. I've just come from Bombay – went down to ship off a drum containing her clothes, record player and typewriter. I managed to go swimming three times in the three days I was there. I find that so relaxing – just floating around in salt water – you can hardly sink.

It's rather hot now, but we had three heavy showers of rain that cooled things off for a few days. It was good to have the dust stop flying for a day at least.

Must go to a tea – I'm at a girls' Bible School for graduation – this is the tea for the senior girls. I will return to Ellichpur on Monday (21st), and there on the 23rd is Hiru's engagement ceremony. Hiru is the sister of Bapurao, and like my daughter for I've cared for her since she was 2 or 3 years old. She will be married on the 24th of April to a very fine Christian boy. Hello to everyone.

Love, Beryl

Pamela Girard

Ramakhera, Dertalai, Nimar Dist., M.P., India
August 28, 1966

Dear Gen and Merle,

I've really been watching the mail for those pictures ever since Ruth wrote that some were taken. They are so good of you all – and of course I was especially anxious to see how Ruth looked. Everyone wants to see them – even little Shimu (3) can point out the "Chati Dadi" the second or younger grandmother. (I'm the first or older grandmother). I think they wouldn't recognize her, however, if they didn't know who to look for. I'm so glad she could be with you a few days – almost as good as being there myself.

I'll be looking forward to your box. My garden is coming on now. I have delicious cucumber salad every night, and had a handful of string beans at noon. I had hoped to be able to can some, but I doubt that I will get enough. Everything is late for the rains were a full month late. Then we didn't even see the sun for 18 days – most everything drowned and had to be replanted. The fields were washed out too – deep gullies torn out all over. Still some fields on higher ground will be okay this year. Around Ellichpur there has been very little rain so there they are again drying out. There seems no way to win in this fight against hunger.

The Kurku Gospel of Mark has at last arrived. Now we must try to get it distributed in every village. This is a tentative edition. I will have to check the response to it in different areas and again revise and then we will print a diglot – Hindi on one side and Kurku on the other.

I'll have to caddy for you when I come on furlough. I don't know the first thing about golf and it has always seemed such a silly game to me to hit that ball as far as you can then carry those heavy clubs off to find the ball! No doubt my education is sadly lacking – huh?

Out of room.

Love, Beryl

Letters From India

(From Ruth Ihrig two years after surgery for brain hemorrhages)

Ramakhera, Dertalai, Nimar District, M.P., India
August 20, 1968

Dear Shirley and Allen,

You would think I ran out of ink or something since I have not written before. These last few months have been so very hard. With Beryl's two operations it being the hot season, etc., I could not have done what I did unless the gracious and faithful presence of the Lord was not with me. I do praise his name. After returning from Bombay, I traveled until 2 – 3 a.m. to get the necessary work done. On July 1st, I got to Ramakhera where we are now.

Beryl got here on the 23rd. Because of the late rains, one of the men, Vern Middleton, could drive the jeep to the river and Beryl only had to walk 2 miles. We didn't know when she was actually coming, but when we saw her, we all ran out into the field to meet her. I couldn't hold back the tears. I was so grateful for what the Lord has done for us both.

We both have both had such serious surgery. Beryl's pain will not disappear for six months – and she has need for special strength as she finds writing one of the hardest jobs ever. Even typing is not as hard, but the Lord is healing her and we do praise the Lord.

We have been grateful the floods, worst in history in some parts, have not hit us. Although, the Tapti River, only a mile away from us, rose 10 feet and caused much flooding in the Gujarat area where so much suffering has been felt.

I was so grateful for the Tecnique Shirley – no duty and so nice to use. I liked the shampoo you sent. I asked my sister to send you some money. Please do use it to send another shampoo. Also if possible could you send a Spun Gold to me? You used this type of thing on some of your ladies *(Shirl is a hair stylist)*, but it is the Tecnique I need. I try not to wash my hair too often so it lasts longer. The Spun Gold is used after shampooing, but comes off on the comb afterwards, but is easy to use. I am so very grateful for these things that help fix up my washed out sun-dried hair! Beryl puts oil on her hair which makes it look nice, but she has dark hair!

With Christian love,
Ruth

Editor's Notes:

Beryl was diagnosed with breast cancer and had radical mastectomies and a hysterectomy. You'll notice it is never mentioned in her letters. Her cancer went into remission and didn't recur until she was retired and living in Minneapolis. It was the eventual cause of her death.

Shirley, a hair stylist kept Ruth supplied with hair dye and shampoo the entire time they were in India. When they were in St. Paul on furlough Shirley always cut and styled their hair. It must have been such a treat for them.

Ramakhera, Dertalai, Nimar District, M.P.
January 8, 1971

Dear Shirl, Al, Cindy and Glen,

New Year's Greetings. May this be a year of really rejoicing in the Lord. Have you noticed how often we are told to rejoice and give thanks? We read, "The joy of the Lord is your strength." And he gives us <u>His joy</u>, John 16:22, 24.

Glad to have your letter. I'm always eager for news.

(January 11) I only got this far. Now I am in the midst of a large Hindu fair. We've set up a book shop, but there is a loud speaker blaring out cinema music close by drowning out ours. So the fellows have taken books and gone off among the crowd to see if they can sell any. I'm sitting here – selling an occasional book. I fear we won't sell much today, and we've come a long way. There are thousands of carts parked all around – many shops, and a circus and cinema – the cinema tents are not yet completely ready it seems. Tomorrow is the main day, I guess. We usually set up tents and stay. This year most of our folks have fields they cannot leave so we are here for the day and may return tomorrow.

Crops are not good this year again. Cotton was destroyed by some kind of blight. Jwar is very poor. Millet is the grain from which poor people make their bread. We wonder how people will make out this year. And now the election is called for the coming March, 1971, instead of 1972 as scheduled. Perhaps congress can come out ahead by this early election. Mrs. Gandhi thinks so and she is very clever.

It is so dusty here that my glasses are constantly filmed over with a coating of fine dust. Looks like a lot of new carnival-type rides are here this year, but I think they are hand run. More later.

Love, Beryl

Ramakhera, Dertalai, Nimar Dist., M.P. India
February 17, 1971

Dear Shirley, Al, and Family,

I think I did write to you since Christmas, but I just reread your last letter and so here is a brief visit via the post. Our mailman has not been here this week so he should surely show up today. Anyway I will have this ready to mail if he does come.

I wonder how Tony is doing, and if he likes the new life he has in the Air Force. I think of him often. Do send me his new address. I just finished a letter to Girard. Maybe I can get one ready for Tony too and you can forward it. Girard is really counting the days till he can return to his Becky.

Our hot season is here, still the last few nights have turned chilly again. In fact it got so cool that I set some Jello. I never have

Jello, but I was hungry for some kind of dessert and thought I would see if it would set. It really tasted good. I can keep things pretty cool by keeping wet towels around a screened box. The winds are high during the hot season and the process of evaporation cools things nicely. Catch is to keep the towels wet all the time.

Glad you are able to attend the morning Bible study. Colossians is a wonderful book. Bapurao has been teaching that here too on Sundays. The only way for a close walk with the Lord is through fellowship with Him in His word and in prayer. For this you must set aside time. I find that I must get up early in the morning to do this.

Ruth hasn't been out for a couple of weeks. Her car needs some working on before she dares to come out on this road. I was in last Friday and saw her. We went to Ellichpur in her station wagon the first of February and on the way back we stopped to let out some folks who had been riding with us. When she came to start up again – the car was dead. I thought the battery cables had probably jumped off. But on further investigation we found that the cable had broken off where it is grounded onto the side. I was able to fix it so that we got back to Dharni safe, but it will need to be welded to really hold on bad roads.

You asked about London? I really enjoyed what I was able to see. I spent most of my time there working on language. But I would have liked time to tour the countryside. I couldn't think at first what made London look so different – after all our cities are similar. Then I realized it was the chimneys. They have no central heating and all those chimneys poking their heads up look so strange to an American. I am sure the parks must be lovely in the summer. In November there were still a few roses left, but not much else. I had a brief trip out into the country to see the home of the missionary I was visiting. Then we returned to London to finish our work.

I am sure you will enjoy your trip to California to visit your sister. I have heard on the radio of the serious earthquake they

Letters From India

have just had in the Los Angeles area. The world is full of tragic happenings.

This will have to be all for now. Just know that I do think of you and miss you all.

Love, Beryl

Ramakhera, Dertalai, Nimar Dist., M.P., India
May 16, 1973

Dear Cindy,

I am not sure of your zip code, but I guess you will get this eventually. I was really pleased to hear from you and know you like school so well, and have a good roommate.

It was -15 when you were writing and now as I am writing it is 110 in my house (118 out on the veranda.) And the wind is blowing a gale of dust and hot air. It has been like this for the last month and we really are wondering when we will get any relief. Many have died of heat exhaustion. I survive by wearing a wet towel around my shoulders and sleeping on one at night. But now the rains are not too far away. In fact it is raining in Assam and the rivers as usual are flooding and causing damage.

The rains in this area (due about June 7) come from the Bombay side and are always later. However because of the intense heat the rains may come early. We hope so for in many places there is no water at all for animals and people stand in line to <u>buy</u> only a small rationed amount. So far this year our wells still have water. Last year they went dry. I believe water must be the most precious thing in the world. No wonder the Bible uses water to illustrate new life – the living word – etc. The Lord promised the Samaritan woman in John 4 to give her Living Water.

I wish you could meet a young Korku girl of this village. Her name is Taru (star). This year she decided that she was going to follow the Lord come what may. She was baptized at our Bible

Pamela Girard

conference. But now the problem comes up about her marriage. If she marries someone who is not a Kurku, the village will no doubt make it very hard for her parents.

She is a beautiful girl. In fact her picture was in my last prayer letter – no doubt your mother has it. There is a young man who wants to marry her, but he is nearly blind. He still can make a living sewing for he is a good tailor. He is a Christian, and his folks are Korkus so there will not be too much objection. But she needs to learn to read well so she can read aloud for their Bible study and would need to learn to help him thread the needle and sew on buttons, etc. His mother does this for him now. Don't know how this will turn out.

I know you have a boy friend too. Be sure you find someone who will want to follow the Lord and be sure that you make that decision yourself. There is no other way to real happiness.

Must make a trip over across the river to where Bapurao and Juli live. They have four boys and this year adopted a baby girl. Her mother died, and when Juli took her, the baby was simply the scrawniest little thing. We weren't sure she would live. Now she is so cute and such a happy baby. Kind of comical too for her hair grows every which way and just around the top of her head. That doesn't matter to her four big brothers. They just love her.

Must close now. I am always interested to hear from and about you.

Lots of love, Aunt Beryl

Editor's Note:

Kurku was also spelled Korku and both were used. However I noticed that Kurku was used primarily in the beginning of her stay and Korku became predominate at the end of her mission.

Ramakhera, Dertalai, Nimar Dist., M.P., India
March 16, 1974

Dear Shirl, Al, and Glen,

It's always so good to receive your newsy letters and to rejoice with you in your desire to grow in your Christian faith. There is always much more to know – deeper to go. Yes, Thes. 5:16-18, I also keep before me at all times. I like the Phillips translation, "Be happy in your faith at all times, never stop praying, be thankful whatever the circumstances may be." You follow this advice you will be working out the will of God expressed to you in Christ Jesus.

Well, I hope you all survive the hockey season. Seems a dangerous sport to me! Course I never did learn to skate. Never had a decent pair of skates for one thing and I understand ice is also necessary – not just the over spill from the water tank.

I just came back from the weekly market. It's only 1½ miles but the sun is terribly hot now. My jeep is not running – throws oil and petrol all over. Besides petrol has gone up again – over $2.00 a gallon so I have to save the petrol for touring in the villages. I really wanted to get tomatoes but there were none. I did get cabbage, green onions, carrots and bananas. This time of year we have quite good markets. But the price of everything keeps going up. Grain is so high that the poor can scarcely feed their family – and work is also hard to find. We keep hearing that there is plenty of grain, but where it is we don't know. How anyone is to buy at these prices is beyond me. Millet is needed for bread, and rice is now too high to buy. And – we hear of famine conditions in Africa.

April 18th – just discovered this letter unfinished. We've had much sickness. I've been on the go helping out. Bapurao had to take his wife to the hospital and I've been staying with 3 boys, one boy and baby girl went with them. Then there has been a very severe epidemic of measles. The children and adults too have been terribly sick. Their mouths and throats are so full of it that they can't eat for 4 – 5 days.

And – on Easter Sunday, Taru had a baby girl at our house at 5:30 a.m. We were up all night with her. So your letter had been forgotten all this time.

It's terribly hot now. Have you read "The Hiding Place" by Carrie Ten Boom? Be sure to get it and send a copy to Cindy. It's a terrific challenge. We do so little for Christ when we read how others have suffered so joyfully.

Love, Beryl

Editor's Note:

Beryl was considered a "midwife helper" but often did most of the work. Many of the village women gave birth on the bare ground. Whenever she was called to help at a birth Beryl brought small blankets to put underneath the mother and wrap the baby. She took great care to follow sanitary procedures as best she could under the circumstances.

Ellichpur, Amravati Dist., M.P., India
May 4, 1974

Dear Precious Ones in Christ,

Thanks a million for your letter – it really thrills our hearts to hear from you! We are at a translator's institute, 7500' high in the hills (mountains?) of South India. As usual Beryl is working hard and learning lots. She sure is a terrific girl, and I have the privilege of working with her! The outstanding thing is how she knows and loves the Lord. Nothing make believe or half way about her.

My prayer is that I will be wholly committed to the Lord always. After all, since the Lord is all He claims to be why not obey and trust Him? We can't lose.

Letters From India

Thanks for the Spun Gold, Shirl. I have to try to stay beautiful you know. It doesn't change the grey, but it does high light what color I do have. When my hair is more truly grey I'll use that bluish grey color grey-haired women use. I think that is pretty. You should know how you helped me look nice at an important meeting in St. Paul. It really did something for my morale. Remember?

I'm in bed under my covers with my clothes on. The temperature is much cooler than the 114 to 115 where we live on the plains. We leave here May 21st.

Again I send my love to you all and also to the nice puppy. Until next time,

Ruth (Ihrig)

Ramakhera, Dertalai, Nimar Dist., M.P., India
September 28, 1976

Dear Shirl, Al and Glen,

My corn bread is about to come out of the oven for supper. I can at least start this letter. I can't remember when I last wrote – am sure it was a long time ago. I was so glad to get your long letter and news.

Since I wrote to you last, Gwen Peck has come to live with me. She was born and raised here in India. Her parents are with our mission and were here in Central India with us until Gwen was about five. Then they were asked to take charge of our Bible College in Calcutta and have been there ever since. Gwen has just finished college and is back for a short stay until May. She majored in anthropology and is here to help type up my cultural notes I have on the Korku people. Right now she is studying the language and part of my time goes into helping her. But now she is able to read with some of the women so that is helping me. I want to get more done on the translation,

Pamela Girard

but have so many interruptions that I don't get enough time to concentrate.

We did not get rain until way into August and then it rained as though it would never stop. We were getting concerned for there are several crops now ready to harvest, and we need sunny days for that. But the last two days have been clear and it seems the rains are over. The worst days are over for the people too. There has been little to eat, but now there is a very small grain-like grass cut. Some if it is very good too. So we hope that there will be crops this year. My garden was not good. Still we have had cucumber salad every night, okra also. The tomatoes are coming on too. So we have had plenty though there are so many to share with that there is not enough left to can.

I just found **all** of your last letter and reread it; so much news. I do hope Cindy made it okay into the Navy *(she did)*. I must write to her. I have not heard from Yvonne for a while, but I do know that the Lord is working there. I had such a nice visit with her and her family. I really do think of you so often, but I have meetings even at night and so I don't get my thoughts down on paper. I will probably come on furlough in '78. But I will stay a little longer this time. Four months go too fast when I have so many churches to visit. It leaves little time to see you all.

Ruth and I are both well. I find it harder to plough through the mud than I used to, but then I am now 59 and I guess I can expect to have to slow down. Last week Gwen and I had to hike out. We waded in knee deep mud through the rice fields that splashed all over us. We were a sight when we reached the main road, but just had time to wash off most of the mud in a muddy stream before the bus came.

After supper Gwen and I went for a walk – three "4 year olds" decided to go with us and jabbered all the time and we were tired out before we got home. I love these little kids and they are here most of the time. When they get to fighting and crying I can always send them home.

I will try to write more often. Remember, "The Joy of the Lord is your strength." Neh. 8:10.

Love to all, Beryl

Ramakhera, Dertalai, Nimar Dist., M.P., India
November 29, 1975

Dear Shirl, Al, and Gen,

Christmas greetings to you all, and to Tony and his wife, and Cindy. I trust this will be a really happy Christmas as you remember our Lord's coming at Bethlehem and look forward to his coming again.

I do think of you often and miss you. Trust you are all well – and happy. Our happiness does not depend upon circumstances, good health, or financial well-being. We are to rejoice always and give thanks in and for all things. Easy? – well not always, but it does bring joy.

It's cold here nights and mornings. I'm wearing a sweater and wool slacks (my feet are always cold.) How the people survive who watch their fields all night is a mystery. Of course they keep a fire burning. It's a difficult time for the poor who have neither warm clothing nor blankets. Grain prices have come down somewhat – but everything else stays high. Folks can barely feed their family, clothing is a problem. Yes, I know it is difficult back there too, especially for those out of work. Yet, the contrast is so great, what are necessities there are luxuries here.

It's hard to know how to help too, so as not to create dependence and jealousy. I try to stick to helping school kids and medical emergencies and that has been a tremendous thing this year. No space left to tell more now. I should have typed.

Love to all, Beryl

Pamela Girard

Editor's note:

After Beryl retired she often spent time with Al and Shirley at their lake cabin. At first she felt hemmed in by the trees, but gradually got used to it. She preferred to be on the lake fishing.

She and Shirl played cutthroat Scrabble games. Al once asked if she would let Shirley win, she replied, "I'm a Girard, and Girards always play to win!" I would occasionally join in but it was humiliating. I started catching on and my score became more respectable. Respectable it may have been, but third I remained.

Shirl told me a story about when she and Beryl went to a Bible camp together. She was so excited that she glowed like a young girl.

Chapter 4

Letters to the World

"Grace and Peace to You From God Our Father and his Son Jesus Christ"
(1 Philippians 1:2)

Ramakhera, Deratalia, Nimar Dist., M.P., India
June 25, 1962

Dear Friends.

Questions, questions all day long!

"Why can't we stay longer?" That was the girls' question at the end of the Bible camp in May. This year we had 19 Hindi speaking girls and 17 Marathi speaking girls. We had a good camp and the girls were not ready to go home at the end of the five days (the teachers were exhausted.) We were pleased to see spiritual growth in some, interest in all, and evidence of answered prayer in the camp as a whole.

"Can't you give her some medicine?" That was the question of the old village mid-wife as I went in to see Jiji bai. She had started labor the day before, and I was concerned. This was her thirteenth child; and only one, Mansaram, who brings our water and helps us, has lived. Most have been still-born or have lived only a few days. We had tried to persuade Jiji bai and David, her husband, to go for treatment last year, but they had not listened. Now it was too late. When I returned in the evening, the mid-wife informed me that a Satan had been born -- not at all human – and they had thrown it out. Poor Jiji bai was sitting up on her bed and David and Mansaram were nearby, sad and bewildered. I explained that this was not Satan, but a disease that could probably be treated if they had only listened. Perhaps this time they will be convinced that the charms of the medicine men are of no avail.

"When will you come to my village? Write down my name, Daya bai; and when you come, ask for my house. You can tell me more about Jesus." Situ bai had brought her to meet us and had then helped witness to her. I camped in her village for a week six or seven years ago and she sang a song she had heard at that time. Well, the meaning was there, though the words had undergone some change. She took several books for her daughter and neighbor to read. "No, she would not let the books get lost."

"When is it going to rain? What do your books say?" Everyone asks this question. The rains are long overdue and still only dust storms. What little feed is left must be kept for the bullocks upon whom the farmer's livelihood depends. The cows are dying. There is very little grain left in the bins for the daily bread. All are concerned. Surely our books must say when it will rain!

"When will you come back?" Bapuroa and Juli with their two small boys are leaving this week for a year of Bible school training. The village folk are sorry to see them go, and we will miss them terribly.

"Will it begin now?" "What will begin now?" – My turn to ask the question of the two shining eyes peering in our window. "The singing!" "No you must come in the evening for the singing." Tomorrow I'll see him peering in my window and hear once more, "Will it begin now – the singing?"

Greetings to you all.

In Christian love, Beryl Girard

Letters From India

Ramakhera, Deratalia, Nimar Dist., M.P., India
August 11, 1962

Dear Friends,

It is a rainy Saturday here in Ramakhera. We needed rain badly, and so we are thankful for it. Also we hope the millions of worms eating our garden and destroying whole fields will be drowned or washed away somehow. I never saw such ugly fellows.

Around 50 children have been here for their daily glass of U.S. powdered milk, and Situ bai has been here to help me for an hour. I'm checking the Korku translation of the gospel of Mark with her right now. Bhaulal has to help with the actual translation, but Situ bai is good at recognizing whether the translation is idiomatic Kurku or not. She also explained the different procedures (male and female) for giving abuse (swearing). A very useful bit of information I thought because it deals with the ancestry of the one being cursed!!

It is also cleaning day. Mansu carried out all the rugs covering our earth-packed floor - - some big some small. The big one is rather faded as we used it for a sunshade once; the crocheted rugs are of all sizes depending upon the number of old saris we had at the time we had the crocheting urge. Probably you would say the colors clash, but when we return to our room after visiting in the villages, it looks like a palace to us. Well, I swept the floor while Mansu shook the rugs bringing them in one at a time. This delays the process, and gives him ample time to check up on whatever I am doing.

It is also baking day in Ramakhera. To save time I try to bake enough for the week. So I am now waiting for a cake to bake and I have mixed up bread. In order to bake today, I had to open another tin of flour. The tin was covered with dust, and so I hunted for rag to wipe it off. In spite of the fact that I hide rags here and there, someone always finds them and I have to look up another. Then I pried off the cover. Inside was another seal upon which was written, "Just pierce here and pry up." I've never gotten the cover off that way and usually end up with the jagged can opener punching into my hand. Well, the cut today was not too deep so not too much time or blood was lost. (I also dislike boxes that say, "Press here." I press and press, and then reach for the butcher knife!

Now my cake is done and I am going to call Mansu to help check some translation work. An hour with him leaves me limp! He squirms. He wiggles. He takes my fountain pen apart. He doodles on pages I have spent hours recopying. And when I ask him something, he stares at me blankly with a "huh?" Yesterday topped the works! I was writing away a bit of information I had pried out of him, when he dropped a scorpion on my page. One stung me recently so I am not on speaking terms with that "jat" (caste) and so I yelped and Mansu laughed. Of course he had removed the stinger. He had four or five like that in his shirt pocket. Rather nerve racking to hear and see how he was pronouncing a difficult word and see a scorpion crawling around on his shirt.

Mansuram is around 16 years old. He has been helping here for two years and you have no doubt guessed that we are pretty fond of him. He does seem to believe in the Lord, and it is amazing how much of the Scriptures he does understand in spite of the difficult Hindi.

And now in case you think this isn't exactly a prayer letter -- well, you are right. This is the personal letter I have always been planning to write to each one of you. It has been just a rambling visit in the time it takes to bake a cake.

In Christian love, Beryl Girard

Letters From India

Ramakhera, Deratalia, Nimar Dist., M.P., India
October 26, 1962

Dear Friends:

"Don't cry. Don't wail. Mae is great!" So the neighbors warned Larki bai. But who can stop a mother's tears when her only son lies dead in her lap, his face so disfigured by smallpox as to be scarcely recognizable.

Smallpox, regarded by the Korkus as the mother goddess, Mae (mother), came to our village in June and is still raging in the worst epidemic we have ever seen. Many of the children died and often the living were left blinded, or with weakened eyes or other complications.

The smallpox goddess herself is supposed to enter into the sick one and even the medicine man bows at the feet of the smallpox victim. We have tried to persuade the Korkus to have their children vaccinated, but more often they hide the children when the vaccinator comes around or bribe him not to vaccinate their child.

Bhaulal, of whom we have written often, had one small son, Premdas, a sweet gentle child whom we all loved. Bhaulal had had him vaccinated; but the vaccine was no doubt old as none of the children vaccinated at that time had positive reactions. Premdas' little playmate came down with smallpox and lay at the point of death for many days. Then slowly he began to recover.

And then Mae came to Bhaulal's house, and it was Premdas who had it. They called us to pray for him. They did not call the medicine man, or make the customary offerings to Mae. Daily we saw the child grow worse until his mouth and throat were also filled with it. Nights were the worst and one night he called out over and over, "I don't want to stay here. Let me go to Father's house." Bhaulal understood him to mean God's house, and so he said, "Go son, go." The next day he told us that he had given him into the Lord's hands. We felt surely the Lord would save the child.

Pamela Girard

But he didn't. He died early one morning just as we reached the house. Bhaulal carried his small son off while we tried to comfort Larki bai and their three girls. On every hand we heard, "They should have done this – or that. Mae is great." Our hearts were heavy as we wondered what would be Bhaulal's and Larki bai's reaction. Other children recovered, but God whom they had trusted had not spared their child.

Our God is great. We thought He would be glorified through the healing of the child. Now through the death of the child Bhaulal has determined to follow the Lord. He is now insisting on his whole family coming on Sundays, and he himself comes on Wednesday for prayer and Bible study. God did not answer our prayers for the child; He saw beyond the child to the need in Bhaulal's own heart, and He is now answering the prayers that have gone up for many years for this man. Many of you pray daily for him and his family. Pray on.

In Christian love,
Ruth Ihrig and Beryl Girard

Ramakhera, Deratalia, Nimar Dist., M.P., India
December 27, 1962

Dear Friends,

Four days before Christmas our house began filling up. Bapuroa and Juli returned from Bible school with their two little boys aged three and one and a half. Our neighbors immediately began dropping in to see them. Even Khanu came and drank a cup of tea with us. The next night the young people of the village came around to see them and to sing. Certainly you would never have recognized the Christmas carols – drum pounding out in typical Korku rhythm and cymbals and tambourines clashing.

On Sunday Jill Bembrick of Gospel Recordings returned to finish recording four new Korku records and to spend Christmas with us. So Monday morning that last record was made with Bhaulal. By the time we had finished, Lilla Kirkpatrick and Janaki bai had arrived from Deratalai. Then even while we were all talking someone called out, "A motor is coming." It had to be Ruth. (This was the first time the jeep had crossed the river after the rains this year.) She had six young Korkus from the Khamla area with her and Bapurao's sister. In the evening Buda with his little daughter and a friend arrived. That Christmas eve we all squeezed into our house to sleep.

On Christmas morning we gathered in a sunny place for our worship service. Some of the young people of the village joined us so we had the largest Christmas service ever held in Ramakhera. In the afternoon Eileen Prickett drove out from Dharni with a jeep load of young people. There were games all afternoon, and at night 40 were present for the evening meal. The fishermen who had promised to supply us with fish for this Christmas khana never showed up; and so we ate ordinary rice and dal (pulse). There was plenty of joshing, "Don't throw the bones on the floor." The amount of food consumed was amazing.

Before we could even clear up after supper, the young people had a sing started. This went on until around 10. By that time we were beginning to feel pretty cold, and so we closed with prayer another Christmas here in Ramakhera.

And now it is nearly 1963. Ruth and I are due to arrive in New York on April 29th on the Queen Mary. We are looking forward to seeing as many of you as possible during our furlough year. We need a furlough, and I guess we look it. Yesterday one of our boys looking down at me exclaimed, "Why, bai, you've gone old!" I started to argue the point, rather half-heartedly, but he reached down and pulled out the particular white hair he had seen and held it before my eyes. But Kamala who was standing by said comfortingly, "My father has white hairs too." And he is – yes, he must be – younger than I.

In Christian love,
Beryl Girard

Pamela Girard

Ramakhera, Deratalia, Nimar Dist., M.P., India
February 20, 1965

Dear Friends:

Ruth and I returned from furlough in June to join Lilla and Eileen in Korku-land. We were thankful to be able to return; the problems are still here, but somehow after a good furlough they do not seem so overwhelming. Besides it is easier for four to face them than two. But then in August Eileen left for furlough. Her dispensary is closed and filled with dust. Daily people ask, "When is she coming back?"

I have given much time to a final revision of Mark. Now only difficult passages remain to be reworked. Lilla is also checking these passages with her Korku informants in Dharni and then joins me in Ramakhera to discuss her findings. On her last visit, however, we spent parts of two days joining in the celebration of Mansaram's wedding. (Now you can include his young bride as you continue to pray for Mansaram.) Another day was taken up in a trip to the court at Burhanpur in connection with the Ramakhera land case. We were quickly relieved of 100 rupees and assured that all was now in order. The case is settled and the land is ours.

Ten or more girls have been coming every evening for several months to learn to read. Seven are doing very well. Now the boys have started to come also. Every evening 15 to 20 children swarm in and demand attention. Few are on the same lesson and since they all want to be taught at once the uproar is tremendous. We can not out shout them so I finally resorted to a stick. A rap on the head or a poke in the ribs restores order. This is the best opportunity we have ever had for child evangelism. Seven nights out of the week they are here and want a story. Do pray that they may really learn who Jesus Christ is, why He came, and what He will do for them.

Christmas at Ramakhera was really the "Big Day". Ruth brought 14 Korkus from Khamla, Lilla met her half way and took part of the load in her jeep. (No wonder the springs in our jeeps are forever breaking!) We had prepared food for 40. Fifty-one sat down to eat and so we had to cook more rice... Afterwards we had pictures and a sing. The highlight of the sing was that we had four new Korku songs.

A few days before Christmas Bhaulal had come to sing a new song for me. It was not very original, but it was his attempt. I wrote it down and then turning to Bhaulal and Yakub who were also present said, "I wish you would write a song to a real Korku tune." Bhaulal said to Yakub, "You do it." Yakub said, "It doesn't come to me." But the next day he did come with a very good song to a Korku tune. Later he did another for Christmas. Then Situ not to be out done by the man made up one and came to sing it to me. After Christmas Yakub wrote four other songs to the tunes of the Korku stick drills. The Korku young men are very clever at beating time by striking each others' stick as they sing and leap in an out. Now we have a group doing it to Christian songs. It is good fun and meaningful too. We ought to leap for joy over what the Lord has done for us.

Bapurao and Juli will be back from school April – June so we are planning for some group touring at that time. We plan to have two Bible camps for Korku children during that time. Lilla is looking forward to furlough in August. In order to be ready for further help and consultation at the Wycliffe Workshop in Mexico, she is spending all available time on the translation of the Gospel of Luke into Korku.

Counting on your prayers.

Beryl and Lilla

Pamela Girard

Ramakhera, Deratalia, Nimar Dist., M.P., India
August 25, 1965

Dear Friends,

This month marks the 20th anniversary of Dora's, Ruth's and my arrival in India. I remember the customs officer who helped us at that time advised us to go back home. He said, "You will lose your youth in India." I presume he was right! No doubt he is still a young man in England.

This month I mailed the Korku Gospel of Mark to the Bible Society for printing. I spent 15 days with the Translations Secretary in June checking through it verse by verse. Then I returned here and went through it again making final corrections and changes. I don't know how many times I have done that; I know I am thankful to have it off my hands. Please pray that it may be ready for distribution in a large fair in January.

This month Dr. Searle has taken charge of the hospital relieving Dr. Powell for furlough. Do remember to pray for him. He will have to work through an interpreter, and that can be very frustrating.

This past week our long draught was broken and the rains have come at last. Now there is hope for some crops though much of the early grain is lost. I was surprised to find some cucumbers hidden away under the big leaves in my garden and so enjoyed my first salad for supper. (Recipe: cucumber, onion, chili pepper, with yogurt poured over the top.)

This month I began working on the Korku-Hindi-English dictionary. It is going to take some time because I type first Korku and Hindi, then change typewriters to do the English. And this is only the first copy. The stencils will be cut from this. As I think of it there's 20 years of work already gone into it; 20 years of language study, Hindi and Korku, and I'm still learning.

Thanks to you for all your faithfulness through these 20 years.

Sincerely in Christ,
Beryl Girard

Ramakhera, Deratalia, Nimar Dist., M.P., India
April 4, 1966

Dear Friends,

On our way to the weekly market to Dharni, I stopped to register some mail. Our postmaster is also headmaster of the primary school. He had planted a little garden in front of the school and post office. As I walked up the path, I spied a beautiful pink rose just opened and paused to enjoy its fragrance. I stopped sniffing, however, when I heard, "She is smelling the flower of the rose, she is smelling the flower of the rose," pass up and down the long rows of students who were watching my approach. As I finished my business with the postmaster, I congratulated him on his garden and the lovely rose. I should have known better. Before I could protest, the rose was torn off and presented to me. Now it would soon be gone, such a lovely thing.

I walked down the road inhaling its fragrance quite oblivious to the various smells around me and the two little girls squatting by the roadside watching me with wide-eyed interest. Back in the jeep I pinned the rose on my sari and felt as though I were dressed for a party instead of heading for a bazaar to sell literature.

We set up our stall by the side of the road, surrounded by carts and bullocks. There Bapurao and the boys began to sing and play and a crowd soon gathered. I sold the books and was glad our first sale was an Urdu New Testament. People pressed in; the wind blew dirt into faces; the sun became hot; and we were thirsty. Still the fragrance of the rose lingered.

Pamela Girard

Later the boys used the phonograph and the Korku records. Then I was free to go see Janki bai, an elderly lady who used to live with us. I had heard about a girl for her son. She was just making tea and I was glad she had put on so much water for I was thirsty. I drank three cups of her tea. I did; but they were awfully small cups.

Then I stopped to see Lydia bai and had another cup of tea, a big one. Bazaar work is thirsty work. On the way back to our stall, I saw a large crowd gathered and edged in to see the attraction. A fellow with a big snake wound around his wrist was collecting a lot of money. I wondered if that would help to sell our books.

Again I sat at the stall while the boys did their marketing. One little boy stood at my elbow staring owl-like, solemn, unblinkingly at me. He was too small to read so I couldn't sell him a book. Finally his older brother called him away. The day was over; a good number of books, mostly Gospels, had been sold into villages we cannot visit; my rose was wilted and so was I. It was time to go home.

Pray for this very important phase of our work – literature distribution.

Sincerely in Christ,
Beryl Girard

Ramakhera, Dertalal, Nimar Dist., M.P., India
December 29, 1970

> "But when the proper time came, God sent His Son, born of a human mother and born under the jurisdiction of the Law, that He might redeem those who were under the authority of the Law and lead us in to becoming, by adoption, true sons of God."
> Galatians 4: 4, 5 (Phillips)

Letters From India

Christmas really starts a month early in Ramakhera when we start reviewing our Christmas songs. Where some of a group do not read and others are only semi-literate, the songs must be repeated over and over until committed to memory. This year since we have several new songs, we decided we should share them with the Dharni church. So we sent word that we were coming to give a program of song. Fourteen or 15 packed into Ruth's station wagon on Christmas Eve for the 15-mile ride. The road looked really horrible at night. At the river we all piled out and Ruth took the jeep up the steep bank alone. The sand is so deep this year we were in doubt as to whether the loaded jeep could climb the bank up out of the river. The practice along the way was really better than the actual performance, but it was a time of blessing to us all to be able to share our joy of the Coming of our Lord.

Christmas Eve was also the day of preparation. While the women cleaned the rice and wheat for the Christmas dinner, the men and children made the streamers to be used in decorating the Christian homes. Takes a lot of persuasion to get five and seven-year-olds to help. And then before we were finished they simply faded away. They were there when I reached for a gob of paste; when I looked up, they were gone. Just at that time, however, Tumala came around the corner and he was enlisted. It is awkward for him to grasp anything as fine as tissue paper for his fingers and thumbs are only stubs. He is a leprosy patient. Finally the streamers were finished and gay and festive they made the yard. I was ready to quit then, but Bhaulal had one more project in mind. He would make a cross to put up and it had to be covered with red paper. I was so thankful to have Bhaulal sober and happy, that I settled down to more pasting.

Christmas morning everyone appeared in new clothes. According to Korku custom new clothes are bought for the whole family once or twice a year at their festivals. So here the new clothes appear at Christmas and Easter. After our morning worship, everyone gathered to help prepare the meal. The men cut up the meat. Some of the women kneaded the whole wheat flour

Pamela Girard

for the puri (flat bread fried in oil), and some ground the spices and chili peppers. Bhaulal bragged, "No one can make puri like my old woman." And we all agreed, much to Larki bai's confusion but delight. The meal was delicious. Then in the evening we had some filmstrips and a good sing, stopping long enough for tea and popcorn balls. Christmas in Ramakhera is a meaningful and happy time as we rejoice in the birth of our Savior.

We have appreciated all your Christmas cards and letters. It is nice to be remembered.

Ruth Ihrig and Beryl Girard

Ramakhera, Deratalia, Nimar Dist., M.P., India
September 25, 1973

Dear Friends,

July is the month most schools open in India. Vacation is over and it's back to the books. From Ramakhera Satyawan and his bride, Sulbha, went to the Bodwad Bible School for his second year – her first. A recent letter brought this word, "We want to witness for the Lord with all our heart and soul."

From Dharni, David, brother of Sundar went to the Sangli Industrial School for his motor mechanic's course. He had never traveled so far before, and was a bit overwhelmed at the thought of going alone. Eileen Prickett took him from Dharni to the railway station. There on the platform was another young fellow headed the same way. So David had a companion. However, this boy went on and David got off the train alone at Sangli. As he left the station to look for a tonga (horse drawn cart) there was another student already seated just hopefully waiting for someone to join him. David wrote, "From Dharni to Sangli school door the Lord did not leave me alone. I have now experienced the Lord's loving care."

We have written about Bishwas, the fisherman, his wife, Venu bai and daughter, Meena now six years old. One day she came home saying, "I need a brother." In July Bishwas and Venu bai adopted a baby boy. The child was so undernourished that his arms and legs were like match sticks. And although he was a year old, he was so weak he could hardly hold up his head. Now after two months of loving care and good food he is getting plump, able to sit up, and at last beginning to stand when helped. Meena likes her little brother, but has a way of disappearing when she is supposed to entertain him.

July and August were very wet months. We have gone from drought to floods. Rain day and night meant no work and the price of grain kept soaring. People were and still are desperately searching for food and the means to secure it. We hope the rice harvest in another three weeks will bring relief.

One Sunday here in Ramakhera our lesson was on giving thanks always. As our meeting closed, the rain settled in to a steady downpour. Soon all the ravines were flooded and overflowing into the fields. We could see that water had covered part of Bhaulal's field; we knew that meant his cotton would be buried under a layer of silt. Bhaulal said, "My field is gone, but I still have Jesus. Let us come together to sing and praise the Lord." Later in September Bhaulal was baptized in the ravine that had flooded his field.

So many of you have inquired about our health that we will close with that report. We praise the Lord for keeping us so well. In fact we think we are doing pretty well considering our age. Of course Ruth claims to be the younger (exactly one month). Maybe that's why Beryl never could keep with her.

In Christian love,
Ruth Ihrig and Beryl Girard

Pamela Girard

Ramakhera, Deratalia, Nimar Dist., M.P., India
February, 1975

Dear Friends,

> "Moment by moment the days swiftly go by,
> Our song is old,
> Come with new ambitions/resolutions
> The New Year has come."

So goes the chorus of one of the favorite songs of our children. For this coming year we here in Ramakhera joined by Ruth and Chamchu and Gudu with two other couples from Khamla, resolved to strive at all times to offer up the sacrifice of praise.

"By Him therefore let us offer the sacrifice of praise to God continually, that is, the fruit of our lips giving thanks to His name." Hebrews 13:15.

And the days go speeding by. It will soon be time for us to pack for furlough. We are coming in mid-April on the excursion fare which gives us 120 days. We know those four months will go mighty fast so we have set up a schedule that we will have to stick to if we are to visit all our supporting churches and friends. It will be something like this:

RUTH	MONTH	BERYL
Wheaton for medicals Illinois Churches	April 15-30	Massachusetts, Pennsylvania, Michigan
Churches in Minnesota, Iowa, Indiana	May	Wheaton for Medicals Minneapolis Area
"	June	North Dakota for rest period
Wyoming, Montana	July	Oregon
Morris, New York	August 1-13	Preparation for return

The area representatives are already in contact with our supporting churches, so we will no doubt have our schedule pretty well set up before we leave India. In the meantime there is still much to do here. February brings our annual Bible camp. The Hindi fairs are starting and that means opportunity for literature distribution. There is still translation to complete, and probably special meetings at Easter.

Thanks for all the Christmas greetings. It is a real joy to hear from so many of you, and your lovely cards make our home colorful and festive. (Next year they will be in other homes.)

In Christian love,
Ruth Ihrig and Beryl Girard

Support needed for Ruth: $65.00 per month	Support needed for Beryl: $15.00 per month
Achlpur, Amravati District Maharashtra, India	Ramakhera, Dertalai Nimar District, M.P, India

August 30, 1975

Dear Friends,

"I had a full day in my purse
When I arose, and now it's gone."

Edgar Guest was accounting for one day, we had a four-month furlough in our pockets when we left Bombay in April and now it is gone. How could it go so quickly?

We were able to visit all our supporting churches and many of our friends and relatives. We were disappointed that time ran out before we could see you all.

It was spring in the east when we arrived and lovely. It was spring when we reached Minneapolis in May and the lilacs were out. When I finally reached North Dakota in June, it was spring there. The lilacs were just blooming and the prairies were covered with wild flowers. Down in New Mexico many of the amazing cactus were still in flower and in Oregon in July the roses were breathtaking. What a beautiful land we have.

We were blessed and encouraged as we fellowshipped with you. We were thankful for your gracious hospitality and kindness, but often overwhelmed at the amount of food at each meal. We marveled at the supermarkets, and were bewildered in the department stores. (Dismayed too to find how easy it is to begin to collect <u>things</u> as our baggage got heavier and heavier.) Beryl was astonished to see a sign, "Flea Market." (She thought it quite likely that she could contribute.) And also surprised to learn that trout like mini marshmallows; Smokey, the Bear is a real bear; and North Dakotans still trap-shoot against a wind approaching cyclone velocity.

Then it was August and we had to be back in India by the 10th. Once again we boarded a jumbo jet (Racket the Korkus call them) and almost like the Magic Carpet were transferred to another culture. We knew we were back in India alright when the boy in front of the American Express building kept shoving an open basket containing a very fat cobra in our faces. (He expected a donation for milk for the poor snake.) Back at Kothara our missionaries were meeting for a day of prayer and we got there in time for the afternoon and evening sessions. Tea time brought a birthday cake for both of us (Beryl's July 19 and Ruth's August 19th).

Now we are settled in and it seems as though we never left. The crows are just as noisy; the dogs bark all night; and the rats are horrible. <u>But</u> we no longer shiver; the children are so cute; and our Christian brothers and sisters welcomed us back. It is good to be <u>home</u>.

In Christian love,

Letters From India

Ruth Ihrig
Achalpur, Amravati
Maharashtra, India

Support needed: $30.00 per month

Beryl Girard
Ramakhera, Dertalai
Nimar District, M.P., India

Support underwritten

Ramakhera, Dertalai, Nimar Dist., M.P., India
1975 Annual Report

As I review the past year, I am struck with the number of first experiences that occurred in my 30 years here in India.

In January for the first time one of our local churches set aside one of their members to be a missionary to the Korkus. They did not choose one of their leaders, but selected under the guidance of the Holy Spirit the young man who was the storekeeper at Kothara. So Pandarang Ingole with his wife and two children came to Ramakhera expressly to learn Korku. In three months he made good progress and then the Kothara church appointed him as an evangelist with special interest in reaching the Korkus in that area.

Pandarang was a good salesman so our literature sales went up as we visited the Hindu fairs and market places. We have completely sold out of the Korku "Life of Christ" and song books. When Ramabhau and I finished checking through the translation of Acts, we took it to Khamla hoping to spot check it here. Chamchu and Gudu were so eager to read more and more, that we spent four days there and read through the book of Acts with them. It was encouraging to find very few words had to be changed for that area.

Then it was April and time for Ruth and me to begin our first mini-furlough. I really do not like rushing from one place to another, but I do like the idea of getting back to our work here more quickly. We will probably be doing this again in 1977.

Back on the job I began typing the translation of Acts for the printers. My goal was set for the end of the year, but I could not foresee the endless interruptions.

Pamela Girard

When I was called in the middle of the night for Taru's second baby, I congratulated myself that we now have a trained Christian nurse in the village. She thought the baby would not come until around noon and so everyone left. When the baby arrived at 6 a.m. I was left alone with Taru and not even a piece of cloth to wrap the baby in. It was a difficult birth and when I had time to look at the child I could understand why. The right arm, shoulder, and breast were grotesquely enlarged. Most of our believers are just out of animism where every disease or abnormality is attributed to evil spirits. I reminded them that the Lord said of the man born blind, "This is that the power of God may be seen in him." We should give thanks for the child, dedicate him to the Lord and give him a good name.

At our Sunday worship Taru and Samuel dedicated him to the Lord. As soon as Taru could walk the four miles to the main road (fifth day), we set out for a mission hospital where there is a skilled surgeon. I also took another Korku child who had a large cyst on her eye. Well, Taru's baby will have to wait for surgery, but the little girl can now open her eye. Sometimes I wonder about all the expense and time involved in these cases. But just last week the father of the little girl sat before me and said, "I haven't told anyone this, but I have been believing in the Lord since we were there at the hospital."

Then it was conference in October. Now we are so few missionaries it is difficult to find someone to do all the jobs that need to be done. Eileen Prickett has been filing the income tax for all of us, but now she was due for furlough. That job was turned over to me. So in the month before Eileen left I tried to learn all the ins and outs of income tax. And the last I saw of Eileen I was still asking, "Just one more question." Well, those of you who know me well know I am an avid reader, but never did my reading run to income tax rules, laws and calculations. And never have I spent so much time and made so many trips trying to locate my police papers. Still do not have them.

At the Christmas holidays we had a team from the Union Biblical Seminary with us. They were of tribal background. The

Letters From India

Santali couple was surprised to find how closely their language is related to Korku. We hope they'll take a vision of Korku work back to their churches.

So the year slipped by. Problems? Yes! But the Lord has been sufficient.

Beryl Girard

Left Top: Buddhist parade in celebration of Buddha's 2500th birthday in Darjeeling. **Left Middle:** Beryl's friend Tumala (or Yohanna), a leper. **Left Bottom**: A beloved dog of a beggar woman. **Middle Right**: Buddhist prayer flags.

Chapter 5

"So I'll Travel Along With a Friend and a Song"

(Wilfred Wilson Gibson)

"Through Rivers and Mud We Creep"
(Beryl Girard)

Ode to a Jeep

"The jeep is a selfish little car,"
Doc Buker wrote to us,
"Your back gets stiff from its awful jar,
And your eyes get full of dust.
It rattles and bangs its body of tin
Till you wonder it doesn't burst,
And as you roll along your purse grows thin,
For the jeep has an awful thirst."

"And what will you do with a load to haul?
Then you are surely out of luck,
For mission work a Jeep's too small,
What you really need is a truck!
And you can't get parts if your jeep should stall,

Pamela Girard

You'll still have to use the bus.
Well, pay up soon – God bless you all!"
Thus wrote the Doc to us.

Now it's very plain to us out here
The jeep's value has not been seen.
For if gas is high, we'll never fear,
The jeep runs on kerosene!
And eight or nine it will safely hold,
A jeep's sides are quite elastic,
Yes, it will take more, I have been told,
But thirteen is really drastic!

Now loading a jeep is quite a stunt,
There's a limit to what you can pack.
Grubbs stacks it high on the hood in front,
Ruth piles it on a rack.
And where can you buy a motor car
That's such a dual purpose hack?
As an ambulance it travels far,
As a hearse with a corpse comes back.

And all through the jungle the village folk
Come running to meet the jeep.
On errands of mercy with a message of hope,
Through rivers and mud we creep.
Where cholera raged in Korku land
Lilla arrived in high speed.
When Katkomb burned, the Khamla band
Rushed help to the folks in need.

And whether we're following an ox-cart road,
Or fording the Tapti River,
Whether we're hauling a mighty load,
Or joy riding in our flivver;
Whether rain or shine, in our heart's a song

> And a gratitude that's deep,
> And we're praising the Lord as we ride along,
> For every single jeep!

Beryl Girard

Editor's Notes:

In a short note to a friend Beryl wrote, "It was in 1947 that word came to us at Ellichpur that there was a sale of US Army jeeps near Poona. Lilla, Ruth, and I with Bill and Grubbsie decided the jeep was better than a bullock cart, and went off to get one each. We had no time to get approval from Chicago. I think Dr. Buker wasn't too pleased – called the jeep a 'selfish little car.' I then wrote this 'Ode' for Doc."

Beryl attended auto mechanics school so she could repair their jeeps. Sometimes it took a lot of ingenuity. In her letters home she would request miscellaneous parts. One letter to her home church, First Baptist in Minneapolis, asked for tires.

On one occasion she thought she had run over a log and stopped to inspect the damage. It turned out to be a very large python which continued its journey across the road.

The jeep proved its usefulness, often carrying passengers that were not expected. When a body was discovered after being in the river three days, the police decided Beryl should deliver the remains to the authorities. I can't imagine its condition.

Pamela Girard

Vern's Lament

Oh, give me a Jeep,
Where the buffalo sleep,
This river's no place
For my Chev.

Oh, give me a Jeep,
My Chev's sunk in deep,
Where only the fish
Ought to live.

Oh, give me a Jeep
With a chain long and sleek
Firmly attached to my Chev.

Hooray for the Jeep,
We're out of the deep.
You're a better car
Than my Chev.

Salam to the Jeep,
As wearily I creep,
Dripping back
To my Chev.

Beryl Girard

Editor's Note:

This was written for Vern Middleton after Beryl pulled him out of the Tapti with "the selfish little car."

Chapter 6
"All Creatures Great and Small"

(Cecil Francis)

"I Hate Rats"
(Beryl Girard)

Rats

The most disagreeable and pesky creature is the rat! I hate rats! They always seem to turn up where I live. They destroy everything. I can't sleep when they are chewing away and so I get up and chase them, but never do catch any. This week I came in out of the village and was looking forward to a good sleep in a bed, first time in three weeks. So I went to bed at 8:30. I had slept about two hours when I heard the rats chewing away. One ran along the rafters over my bed and one scampered behind a box where I couldn't get at him. I was just plain mad. I went back to bed, but got up several times to cover up things I didn't want chewed.

Finally I got out a tube of rat poison and read the directions. It was supposed to be put on bread. I didn't have any so crawled back into bed leaving the tube of rat poison on the desk. Again

I heard the chewing and then a rat ran under my bed dragging something. I turned on my flashlight to see and there the dumb rat had chewed two holes into the tube. I thought okay fellow that is just good enough for you and finally went back to sleep with the rat eating the poison under my bed. In the morning there lay the rat and the rest of the poison. Last night not a single rat came around to bother me.

Jungle Cats and Jackals

There are panthers and tigers around too. I just heard that a panther killed a man three days back. Not long ago a huge leopard walked slowly across the road right in front of my jeep. When we are camping in our tent the jackals make an awful racket.

Indian Black Bear

The bear is the most dangerous animal in the jungle. He is just plain ugly and is always attacking men who cut wood in the jungle. They stick to the densely wooded area though and so there are not so many around here. When I go back to Katkomb, I can always see signs of them.

The Shrew

The pesky little shrew keeps me awake. The shrew is blind and always runs along the edge of my tent never venturing into the middle. He squeaks as he runs and always when he is right behind me and nearly scares the wits out of me. He has a long pointed nose that wiggles and twitches and he pokes into everything.

Spiders

Every morning before I begin my translation work, I make an inspection of the garden. Each flower has to be admired and thanks given to the Lord for the pleasure He gives through my garden. It was zinnia time and the balsam were still lovely. Then I noticed on one balsam what appeared to be a yellow bud, but I have no yellow balsam! So I dropped down to examine it, and found a most interesting spider. Its body was a lovely lemon cream color. It was crouched on its 4 back legs and held both front legs up in a pincer fashion, ready to catch any fly that came along. I watched for some time, but it never moved. Later as I returned from my inspection, he had a big fly.

In the next few days I discovered 3 or 4 more – all different colors, milky white, pale green, another green with brownish bands. One lived for several days on a big zinnia, and I was horrified to find one morning that my innocent little spider had caught a beautiful big moth (moths are rather stupid creatures after all).

The pale yellow one disappeared – so did the white one. Others moved – evidently they could spin one long strand to swing from one vantage point to another. I thought one of the hawk moths had captured my crab spider, but on closer examination, I saw it was the hawk moth was the captive!! Finally all disappeared, and I felt lonesome without them.

Snails

This year the coleus seeds I planted did not come up. I was disappointed for I am very fond of the coleus – so individualistic. Then one day I found one tiny plant in the garden. I was so pleased that the Lord had given me one. I immediately transplanted it and watched it to ward off any danger. It nearly drowned once, then just as it was coming along nicely, I discovered something was eating it!!! It was then that I found the snails. Some were so tiny that I needed my magnifying glass to see them. Obviously they had to be removed from the coleus so I fixed a nice jar of mud and leaves and brought them in the house where I could watch them. A more interesting family I never had!

Flies

It was fly season and the Sunday school children were meeting on the veranda. We were pasting pictures in books, but the flies were swarming around and in the paste. Jimu, the four-year-old, took a gob of paste on his finger. Immediately a big fat fly sat in it – stuck fast. Jimu held up that small finger for me to see and to call my attention to his problem called out, "Dadi, Dadi' (Grandmother). So I removed the fly and he got the paste on his picture and into the book with no further mishap.

Flying Fox
(Written after retirement)

Last night I watched a program where scientists were searching for the source of one of the deadly diseases now in China and other eastern countries. They finally came up with the carrier – the flying fox.

Interesting for in India I often saw the flying fox hanging (upside down) in the jungle where we were camping or passing through. In the night they fly – darting here and there seeking food. They are really beautiful and interesting creatures, bat-like but larger with reddish fur and a fox-like face. The Korkus have a story about the flying fox.

"The flying fox felt isolated so they went to the birds asking to join their community. The birds said, 'Well you have wings and you fly, but you give birth to your young and have fur. No, you can't live with us.'

The flying fox went to the animals. 'No, you do have fur and give birth to your young but you have wings and you fly! No you can't live with us.'

So the poor little creature feeling so ashamed flew off into the forest and began hanging upside down in the trees all day and flying around for food at night."

Birds

The birds here in India are very brightly colored, many tiny green birds, a green pigeon, green parrots, blue jays, and birds of paradise with long tails. Our robin here does not have a red breast, but is a small saucy little bird with a jaunty tail and the red spot is under his tail.

In the early morning or late evening you can hear the peacocks. Now for all their bright feathers and long beautiful tails the peacock can't sing a note. They make a honking noise and then again they meow almost like a cat.

And then if you lie on your back and look up into the blue, blue sky and if your eyes are sharp you may see just a tiny speck circling around far, far away. That is the vulture. On the ground the vulture is the most hideous looking bird about the size of a turkey, with a bald head and long skinny neck. It runs with a funny sort of lope, but in the air the vulture is the most graceful of birds. What is it doing up there ever circling? Why it is watching far below and if it sees anything dead or dying it will immediately drop down for a feast.

Oscar the Shrew
(A Children's Story)

This the first day of July, 1954 seems like a good day for me, Oscar III, to begin a record of my experiences with my mis-sahib. It came about in this way that three generations of the shrew family have been in the service of our mis-sahib the missionary lady camped in the village of Katkomb. Her tent was pitched under a big tree there.

My grandfather, Oscar I, was working the fields of one of the Christians named Unas. Grandfather, Oscar I, had a very curious nature. He was also a gentleman, so he went to call on the lady from America. He entered by the door and squeaked politely, "Salem". The mis-sahib jumped about a foot in the air according to Grandfather. She didn't seem friendly, but everyday Grandfather went to call on her anyway and helped himself to some of her food.

The miss-sahib was very cross and always told him to go away, until a certain event occurred. One night as mis-sahib was going to bed, Grandfather noticed that old Bitchu (scorpion) was curled up in the foreigner's bed, but she didn't see him there. So Grandfather ran right up behind her and squeaked as only a shrew can squeak. She jumped up and reached for a cane to chase Grandfather. And then she saw old Bitchu.

The next day when Grandfather arrived in her tent, there were a bunch of boys there (little savages they were too). They all took after Grandfather, but the mis-sahib said, "No, leave him alone, he saved me from old Bitchu last night." From that night on, Grandfather moved in and adopted the foreign lady as his mis-sahib. She gave him the name Oscar, and used to talk to him when no one was around. She said he was the only one there who could understand English! So that his how our service began, Grandfather, then Father, and now me, Oscar, III.

The Birthday Party
(A Children's Story)

It was a beautiful day in India. The sky above was so blue and the clouds were such a fleecy white that even a zebra couldn't look at them without squinting a bit. But it was a beautiful day for another reason for it was the little zebra's birthday and there was going to be a party. Yes, that's right. He was now one year old and all the children of the zoo were coming, and there would be games and presents and good things to eat.

The keeper of the zoo had made arrangements for all the young animals to come to the big green square in the middle of the zoo. Oh, the little zebra was so excited that he couldn't sleep all night, and now he just danced around and kept pestering his mother so much by asking her what time it was that he made her nervous. Finally she said, "You go get cleaned up for the party." My, how he scrubbed so that his white stripes were very, very white and his black stripes were very, very black. He really was a very pretty little boy, but his mother didn't tell him so for fear he would get proud.

Then the youngsters began to come. First of all came the elephant with his very wrinkled coat and big feet, and right behind him was the new little giraffe girl with a bright blue ribbon around her neck. Zebra thought her coat was very pretty and she moved very gracefully though she never would say a single word, she was so shy and bashful.

They each brought him a little present, the elephant a bag of peanuts and the giraffe some very tender juicy leaves. Then there was the bear cub in his warm coat; he brought a nice sweet potato. The leopard cub and the tiger cub arrived all dusty and dirty for along the way they had quarreled and had rolled over and over in the dust. The little hippo had a very clean face, but his feet were sort of muddy, and the sad-eyed little buffalo was spick and span. All of them brought the best gift they could. Oh there were so many small animals and they all began to play games. They had such fun.

Then all of a sudden the tiger cub, who was sort of a smart-aleck saw another small animal standing on the side watching. He didn't belong in the zoo at all. He had long ears and a very shabby coat. He was pretty small. "A little runt," thought the other animals, and he certainly wasn't very pretty. His eyes were big and sad, and he was lonely.

"Hey, kids, look who is here," called the cub. "Guess he is trying to break into our party." Then all the children began to make fun of the poor little stranger. He tried to run away, but the animals had surrounded him and there he stood trembling and afraid. "Yeah, look at his long ears," called one and another looked at his droopy tail and the baby zebra smiled smugly as he looked at his own smooth shiny coat. "His mother brings our food to the gardens every day," said the little bear. "How come he is invited to the party?" They made such a noise that the mother and the keeper and other animals came to find out what was going on. The mother zebra saw at once what was happening and scolded the children for being so rude to the little stranger. Then she called them all around her and made them sit down for a story.

And here is the story she told them, "In the beginning God made the heavens and the earth. He made the heavens and the dry land and the grass that grows and the trees. Then he made the sun and the moon and the stars. After that came the birds and the creeping things."

"Me, too," asked the little crocodile?" "Yes, you too," said the mama zebra with a smile. "Then he made all the animals. All of you God made just like you are, the giraffes with a long neck so that they can eat out of a tall tree and spotted so that they can hide in the shadows and no one can see them. He made the elephant with a long trunk so that they can reach out and tear off the grass they like to eat and the bear with the sharp claws so that he can dig for the roots and things he likes to eat.

Then He made a man in His own image and gave man the job of looking after all the things in the garden He had made. Man was supposed to be the master, but all of us animals were supposed to help him. His name was Adam and his wife's name was Eve. Then Adam gave us all our names. We were all so happy there in the garden for a long time.

Then one day Adam and Eve disobeyed God and He had to turn them out of the garden. After that nothing was the same. The animals began to kill and destroy and man had to work very hard to make a living. But you know that way back then God promised to send a Redeemer, a Saviour into the world who would save man from his sin and would then restore the animals and everything to the way it was before the Lord had to close up that Garden of Eden.

Well, for many, many years everyone watched and waited for the Saviour to come. Then one night He came, and came in the form of a man baby and was born in a manger in Bethlehem. Not any of us beautiful animals were there, but I think maybe this sad and lonely creature's grandparents were there for they are the folks who lived in the stable. Then all the baby animals turned to look at the funny little creature with the long ears and the white nose. They wished they might have been there to see the baby Jesus, for that is the name of the Saviour who came.

"Is that the end of the story!" asked the little zebra. "No, said his mother." Then she continued, "When Jesus became a man He went about doing good and healing those who were sick and telling people to repent of their sins and turn to God." Then one day the people wanted to make Him King and so He went up to the city called Jerusalem. This time He did not walk, but sent His disciples to bring Him an animal that He might ride into the city. What animal do you think He chose?"

"I guess He choose us", said the elephant for in India all the great raja ride on the elephant. "And the little white colt, jumped up and said, "No, He didn't for all kings ride on white horses – so there." Then there really did begin an argument for the camel also claimed to be the King's choice.

"No," said the mother with a smile as she drew the lonely little stranger into the circle, "He rode into Jerusalem on the donkey."

"He did?" cried all the animals in surprise. Then they looked at the little donkey and wished they had not been so mean to him. "He did?" said the little donkey and big tears rolled down his little hairy face onto his shiny little nose and dropped off onto the ground. My, he was glad he was a donkey now.

"Then the Lord Jesus died on the cross to save all who will believe in Him from their sins. But he didn't stay dead for He rose from the grave the third day and is now in Heaven." All the little folk looked up then at the bright blue sky trying to see behind the clouds. Then the mother went on, "But some day He is coming back again and then all of us animals will be friendly again. The lamb will lie down by the lion and go to sleep and you children will be kind to one another."

Pamela Girard

"Now that is the end of the story for now. Run and play while I fix your lunch." And away they all scampered, laughing, and pushing, and in their midst was the little donkey as happy as any of them – no even happier I think. And when he went home that night he held his head very high; yes, very high indeed.

Beryl Girard

Chapter 7
"Suffer the Children to Come Unto Me"

(Mark 10:14)

*"I very sad am, my heart very sad is.
But I in hell was and in darkness was,
but now, mis-sahib ji, I very many thanks to give.
You me in the light and on the road to heaven did place."*

(Letter from Sukhalal to Beryl during furlough)

Sukhalal

He was just another little black-eyed brown baby to the village of Katkamb, but to the young mother he was a precious jewel, and so she named him "Sukh," joy, and "Lal," jewel, Sukhalal, a jewel of joy. Sukhalal's first days were spent close by his mother's side. If he so much as whimpered he was immediately snatched up and nursed and lulled back to sleep.

Every day his mother sat down with her legs stretched out straight before her. When laying her fat little baby on her legs she scooped up the warm water from the earthen vessel beside her and poured it over her squirming baby. After his bath she rubbed coconut oil into his soft brown body. Oh, how he did enjoy that! Around his waist she tied a thread that was to ward off evil spirits and around his tiny wrist the bracelets. His mother then caught first one little fist that was waving so threateningly in the air and then the other and squeezed them through the sleeves of a wee jacket; on his head went the little cap that all Indian babies wear and need to protect their ears. Then into his swing he went – a rope stretched double across the room of the tiny hut into which a blanket was folded over and under and inside out to make a neat little hammock -and so off to sleep.

When he was able to crawl, Sukhalal began to explore. Around he went on the mud floor, smooth and clean from a fresh coating of cow dung. In the center of the floor sat his mother in her bright red dress, five yards of material tied at the waist, wound round for a skirt, up over the head, and down the front for an apron and a big pocket. She wore such a lot of bright jewelry, too; bracelets, rings on her fingers, in her ears and one in her nose. He could always hear the clink of her big brass anklets and the tinkle of her toe-rings as she climbed the hill from the well balancing the two big water pots on her head.

Now she was lifting high a heavy wooden club and dropping it on the rice in the hole in the floor. So that was what that hole was for! Sukhalal had wondered as he had stuck both tiny feet into it the day before. His mother was polishing the rice. And this thing in the corner he liked. His mother turned it "round and round" and a fine dust came out. He couldn't even budge the heavy stone, but the wooden handle was fine to help him stand up. His mother called it a chuki (mill) and from the fine dust she made bread.

One day he stood up all alone and everyone laughed and praised him so that he tried it again; then with one foot before the other he began to walk. His young mother snatched him up and proudly called the neighbors to see. After that it was easy and he could explore further abroad. Now he went all around his tiny home. The walls of woven bamboo were plastered over with mud; here and there the mud had cracked letting the sunlight stream through. The roof above was thatched with grass, and he could

Letters From India

see the bright eyes of a big rat peering down at him as it ran across the beams. The roof was full of rats in the day time; at night they ran around the floor over the sleeping people.

In the center of the room were the big grain bins that his mother had made out of the mud and straw that she mixed together with her feet, then built up by hand and dried in the sun. Beyond that in the darkest corner was the stove. He'd watched his mother make that too, mud and dung built into the shape of horse-shoes about 12 inches high. He liked the bright embers and the flame, but the smoke that filled the room made him cry. Under that was a basket with a mother hen. He wouldn't molest her now; yesterday he had learned that she resented little boys.

Now, what was his mother going to do? Ohoho, she is kneading the flour for bread. Now she rolls a big ball of dough round and round her hands. Oh, it is getting bigger and rounder and flatter. So big it is! There she has flopped it on the griddle and starts another. She had better turn it over or it will burn. Now it is done, and she scrapes some of the embers out in front of the fireplace and lays the hot bread on it. Um, will it be good and crusty; just right for a little boy to chew.

Sukhalal's days sped by playing in the sun with the other children, a dirty little boy for now there is no time for mother to give him his daily bath. Father is a farmer and works hard to make a meager living, and mother must help him too. Sukhalal is supposed to watch the house while they are away. He is beginning to learn that life is hard out in the jungle; sickness, danger, death lurk around every corner and the darkness is full of evil spirits.

The cold fever (malaria) that first sends the terrible coldness up your back causing you to shiver and shake until you can't get warm no matter how many blankets you have, then breaks out in a burning fever with a terrible headache and backache and sometimes vomiting and diarrhea come again and again. His mother put some more egg shells on the stick over-head to keep out the evil spirits that brought the fever. Arki (pink-eye), colds, and mats (smallpox) swept the village. Many of his playmates died, and he could hear the wail of the women as the men carried the tiny bodies out to the Kurku burial ground.

One day he went into the darkened end of the veranda to get the egg that surgi (the hen) was bragging about, but as he reached into the dark, up raised the hooded head of Nag, the black cobra. Back he ran screaming, "Ma, Ma, samp (snake)". His mother called Unas (Jonah), the Christian, who was a great hunter, and he came with his gun and shot the big cobra.

Then it was time to start school, and off he went with the other boys. Most of the children were Hindis, but there was John, the son of a Christian, Nu (Noah), and a few of the Kurku boys. Now he began to learn, not his mother tongue, Kurku, but Hindi the language of the Hindus. Every day he laboriously wrote on his tiny slate and recited in unison with the other boys. School wasn't much fun. He much preferred sitting at the feet of his old granny while she told him the legends of the Kurku people. He knew that the Hindu children made fun of the Kurku children, but his old granny told him that the Kurkus were the first people to live in India and how they had once roamed over the land. When the invading Aryans came in from the north, however, the tribe peoples were driven back into the hills. "But," said granny with a smile, "we have never been slaves to anyone as have the proud Hindus." After that Suklalal, too, began to walk with the same independent swagger so typical of the Kurku men.

School was now over for Sukhalal as it is for most Kurku lads. His father needed him, and he began the lonely task of watching the village cattle all day long in the jungle. Off he and his companion would go in the early morning, two small boys with their axes over their shoulders. It was a lonely task; sometimes they made little carts out of grass and bamboo; sometimes they slept in the shade. Often they would see a jungle animal. The monkeys warned them with their whoop when a tiger was around and the boys clutched their axes as they rounded up the cattle. The animal they most feared was not the tiger or leopard, however, but the big black bear. When the peacocks began to honk in the evening, they headed the herd for home.

Sukhalal knew that there were many different castes in Katkomb. There were the Moslems, the Kindus, three families of Christians and the Kurkus. The Moslems looked with distrust on the Hindus with their many gods, the Hindus despised the Kurkus; the Christians lived apart from them all, refusing to bow down to the many gods of the Hindus. The Christians could all read, and they read from a big book and sang many songs. They had one festival, the Great Day (Christmas). The Kurkus worshipped stones and evil spirits. Most of the boys were afraid of the Bhumka, the Kurku medicine man who could drive out evil spirits.

One day the sound of a motor was heard in the village. Many times the village people had heard a motor and had learned to recognize the huge bird-like machine that flew over their village as an air-ship. But this was different, and soon all the children, men and women gathered in the village square to watch the little motor slowly approaching. It stopped before the house of the Christians and out of the jeep-car piled Hindustani folk and two white faced women. The village people pressed and crowded around staring. After that visit they came again and again. They told of a God who cared and loved even the Kurkus and Who was the Saviour of the world. Suklalal asked the Christian Immanuel more about this matter.

The hot season came and with it the "loo", the strong burning wind of the hot season. It was market day in the near-by village, and most of the men were gone. A little girl started her fire to bake the evening bread; the strong wind swirled in and around sending the flames racing up the walls and into the grass roof. Then driven by the wind the hungry flames devoured house after house as the entire village blazed. There was no one to stop it and the well was far below the village. The men returned at night to find only charred and smoking ruins. Again the white-faced people came, Christians from another land, and the people clustered about them, tearful, silent, bewildered. The grain bins that had been full were broken open and the grain lay smoldering. The brass water pots were twisted and melted. Nothing remained.

Pamela Girard

Slowly the men began to stir. The rainy season was at hand and temporary shelter had to go up. The news spread rapidly that the mis-sahibs (missionaries) would also build a house and live in Katkomb.

It was a nice little house that the mis-sahib came to live in, mud walls, grass roof, and a tiny garden out behind. Sukhalal came to work for her, to cut the wood and haul the water, and to accompany her on the long treks through the jungle. Every day he sat down with John and Maiti to study the Bible and memorize the verses the mis-sahib gave him. He learned that the God Who made the world and Who made the Kurkus is not a god of stone, but a living personal Saviour, the Lord Jesus Christ. He believed in this Saviour and began to pray to Him and to witness to the others as he accompanied the mis-sahib from village to village. He taught his parents all that he learned and insisted that they learn to thank the Lord for their food before they ate.

Every night the mis-sahib came to his house and taught his parents. She spoke in Hindi, but when she had finished then Suklalal told them over again the same story in Kurku. And they gladly heard Sukhalal's mother say, "If Sukhalal becomes a Christian, I will too!" But she talked too much. The headman of the village, Hindu, heard and came to threaten. "We will drive you out of the village if you become Christians. Stay away from the Christians, don't read the Bible, and don't close your eyes when you pray." Sukhalal's father listened. He made Sukhalal stop working for the mis-sahib and later he beat Sukhalal's mother with a club so that the blood streamed from her head. He accused the Christian, Immanuel. He threatened to burn Sukhalal's Bible and forbade him to read it.

That night as the mis-sahibs lay in their tent and the village people slept in their houses, an animal began to roar. It came closer and closer; the mis-sahibs lit their lantern and prayed. The monkeys in the jungle called excitedly to warn the other jungle folk, and the cattle crowded together snorting and nervous. The Hindus said it was the devil; the Kurkus knew it was a tiger and some of the men went out with torches to frighten it away. Sukhalal lay sleepless and lonely in his home, planning.

Two days after the mis-sahib left, Sukhalal followed. He found her packing to move, and told her that he had left home. "I want to be baptized," he said. In vain she tried to persuade him to return to the village and witness there; but he always replied, "I can't read the Bible in my home. My father has tried to burn it, I won't go back." Now, the mis-sahib did need a boy to drive the oxen to move her miles or so up and across the river, and so it was agreed that Sukhalal would help her move and then she would help him to get a job on a building project. The way was long and the sun was hot. The mis-sahib dozed, but Sukhalal and the mis-sahib's little companion Dyawanti talked. Said Sukhalal, "I am not going to work on that house." "Well, what are you going to do then?" questioned Dyawanti. "I am going to help the mis-sahib preach the Gospel to the Kurkus." The mis-sahib said no more about the building project.

The first thing the mis-sahib learned at Dharni before moving across the river was that the police were looking for her and Sukhalal. His father had turned in a report that the mis-sahib had taken his 15-year old boy and wanted the police to bring him back. All knew that Sukhalal was more than 15, and so the little party in the covered oxen cart moved on over across the Tapti river to a place so inaccessible that the police never molested them. And it was there that Sukhalal began to witness in earnest for the Lord. Everyday the three Christians – Sukhalal, Dyawanti, and the mis-sahib, sat together and studied. Then in the afternoon and evening the boy repeated in Kurku what he had learned in Hindi, and the people listened as they heard the Gospel story for the first time in their own tongue.

But Sukhalal wanted to be baptized. The only question that remained was that of the police. The Indian law forbids anyone under sixteen to change their religion with out the consent of their parents. His father said Sukhalal was 15 and so under age, but others said he was 18 or 19. Finally the mis-sahib went off to the police station to see if they would permit her to see the records and so learn how old he really was. Of course, the police did not help her and so back she went to the jungle.

Across the Tapti were now 4 mis-sahibs and one sahib (man missionary) and his mem-sahib (wife). All agreed to go ahead with the baptism and to hold it in a central village. The village people were invited and many came to watch. It was a great day for all. Sukhalal had never seen a baptism; Pane, the evangelist, had never baptized anyone, and the missionaries had not seen one of the Kurkus baptized. Sukhalal was the first of his people out in the jungle to step out for the Lord.

Forming a procession they marched down to the river singing as they went the Gospel songs in the Kurku language. On the banks they paused while Pane explained the meaning of baptism. Then he led Sukhalal into the water, and the boy turned to give his testimony. He began to speak in Hindi, but the men on the banks called, "Speak in Kurku," and in his own mother tongue he gave his testimony of how he had turned from the worship of stones and evil spirits to the living God, Jesus Christ. Then Pannu baptized him; and as he came up out of the water, it seemed that his face shown like that of the martyr Stephen, like that of an angel. He is not a handsome boy, but to one mis-sahib at least he was beautiful that day.

The story of Sukhalal does not end there; it is still going on as he continues to witness in the villages. He is just a simple jungle boy, not overly ambitious, not at all well-educated, but I believe he does love the Lord and I would ask all who read his story to pray for him.

Written sometime in December, 1950

Baparao

You would all like Baparao, the boy who has come to live with me and help in the work. His mother and father both died last year and so he came to live with a Christian uncle. Since his uncle already had a whole houseful of children of his own, he was very glad to send Baparao out here into the jungle with me. He is about

14, a nice looking boy with laughing brown eyes (most everyone in India has black eyes).

He is supposed to cook the noon meal while the rest of us are away witnessing or teaching in the villages. Of course he is just learning to cook and so sometimes his rice is damp and soggy instead of dry and fluffy as it ought to be and his bread is sort of hard, but it gets better each time he tries. He does love to tease the old Bible woman, Yohanna bai, whom he calls granny. But she gets even with him by calling him "fat".

He was saved after he came to live with me. When I was telling him about the Lord, I tried to show him that he was a sinner. He declared that he had never sinned. Finally I said, "Well, then Jesus did not die for you for He died just for sinners." He knew that Jesus must have died to save him too and so that very night he asked the Lord to forgive him and to save him. Since then he has been baptized and now when everyone comes to the tent while we are away in the village he tells them about the Lord. His language is Marothi and out here we all speak Hindi. I have been trying to teach him Hindi, but it is slow work and he makes many mistakes. We all laugh as we remember how he told me that there was a man outside who wanted an "election". He meant an injection.

Written February 2, 1952

Tukaru

Tukaru lives in the village of Katkomb. He is probably about 10 or 11 years old. They never know how old, and it is hard to guess because they are usually much smaller than boys back home. When I first went to the village to live in the little mud house, he was one of the low caste and so the other children wouldn't have much to do with him, but he was a nice little boy with a big mole on his chin, brown eyes and a sweet smile.

Pamela Girard

He learned very fast as I told him the stories about our Lord. Then one day he bowed his head and asked the Lord Jesus to take away his sin. He learned to pray and memorized the verses as fast as he could, but you see he couldn't read and so he would only learn while I was there to teach him.

Soon I moved on to another village, but always when I came back Takaru was the first person to greet me. I asked him if he prayed and trusted in the Lord and he said he did, then I asked him to say some of the verses that he learned, and you must understand that I had not seen him for nearly two years and there had been no one else there to teach him, but he could say all of the verses that he had learned.

His father has died and now he must do much of the field work. There is no time for him to go to school to learn to read. I would like to get back there to teach him, but there are so many villages to go to and there are not enough Christians to go around.

We pray that the Lord will send us more missionaries.

Written November 21, 1951

Letters From India

Champa Lal

What is this that I am seeing?
What a tiny restless being!
Now on one foot blindly hopping,
Ever twirling, never stopping,
Round and round, his shirt tail flying
Now exhausted, still he's lying.
And he's quiet for a time.

Now my doorway he is nearing,
Through the dimness shyly peering,
At my smile he answers grinning,
Now more boldness he is winning,
Around about now staring, looking
Watching while the mis-sahib's cooking
And his eyes with wonder shine.

By my side now squatting, listening
Hearing, seeing, eyes glistening,
Leaning on me, not now fearing,
Of the Savior he is hearing.
How He dwelt here, living, dying,
With His blood our pardon buying.
How today He's living, saving
All who are salvation craving,
Who-so-ever will believe.

As I'm speaking, hoping, praying,
That his thoughts will not be straying,
Praying that this child believing,
In his heart Christ now receiving,
Hoping that I'll hear him saying,
As he pauses in his playing
"On the Lord I do believe."

Written during November, 1949

Chapter 8
Meditations on Scripture

*"The Lord will watch over your coming
and going both now and forever more."*
(Psalm 121:8)

It was the end of the hot season in Central India. Soon the rains would come and we (Ruth and I) needed to move back to our home across the Tapti River. The road into this hill station in the Satpura Range would soon become impassable. Yet I wanted to visit another hill village, Makhla, to check the Korku translation I was working on. I could see the hill from the top of Khamla – some 15 miles cross country with a valley in between - by the main road some 30 miles. I would use the cross country road down one mountain side and up the other. I read Psalm 121 and committed this to the lord. Then I went to help pack the trailer. Two young lads, Bapurao and John would need a tent, and I would use the pup tent.

We started off. The road wound round the hills on the very edge of the cliff. Then we came to a rock slide. The road was blocked. No way could we turn around or back up. We started throwing rocks over the edge. Finally I thought we could squeeze by, and didn't breathe nor look down until we were safely past. "He will not let your foot slip" (or jeep).

Next problem after reaching the village was finding shade for our tents. Some distance from the village we found a couple of trees. Though the hills are covered with a teak wood forest, the jungle of Central India, the tops of the hills are bare. And in India the trees shed their leaves at the beginning of the hot season. So we pitched our tents there. "The Lord watches over you. The Lord is your shade. The sun will not harm you by day nor the moon by night."

I spent the day with Kurku friends going over the Korku translation. By night I was exhausted and crept thankfully into my pup tent. It was small so if I stretched out either my head or feet were outside of the tent. The moon was full and beautiful so I lay with my head out and fell asleep. I was awakened by a rustling in the lantana bushes behind my tent. Then I heard a woofing sound....Bear! Now the bear is the most dangerous animal in the jungle. The tiger seldom attacks man, but the bear may attack with no provocation. I pulled myself inside the tent and closed the flap – no way could it be secure against the bear if he wanted to enter. For awhile I sat listening but I was so weary. Then I remembered, "The Lord will keep you from all harm; He will watch over your life. He who watches over you will neither slumber nor sleep." No use both of us staying awake, I thought, and so I went to sleep.

The next day we returned to Khamla taking the long way round, the main road, singing thankfully as we went. "The Lord will watch over your coming and going both now and forevermore." And so we were safely home.

"Use hospitality one to another without grudging."
(1 Peter 4:9)

This is so important in trying to reach our neighbors, or in helping new believers. We make it difficult because we feel we must spend all forenoon preparing a big dinner, or maybe you just can't afford a fancy meal. Whatever happened to old fashioned baked beans? Or even tinned beans? Or pancakes?

One day I visited Munji and Leela's home. They wanted me to share their meal of ghata (cracked millet steamed fluffy), the common meal of the Korkus. I was reminded of Uncle Louis in "Such a Life" by Edith Lazenbnik. "We got what we got," Uncle Louis said, "When we got beans, beans you got." So Leela dished up the ghata for me with a very watery spiced lentil. "When you got ghata, ghata you got." So we all ate and it was good. I refused a second helping not because I was full, nor because I didn't like it, but Munji looked awfully thin. Ghata beans are delicious when you are hungry. Obviously he had not been eating much ghata lately. Jesus taught, "It is more blessed to give, then to receive." If you've got beans (or ghata) those beans shared taste better.

"Open your homes to each other without complaining."
((1 Peter 4:9-10)

I sat cross-legged on the earthen floor in a Korku home (in central India). The earthen grain bin behind me made a good backrest. Since I was facing the fireplace, I could watch Immanuel's wife and teenage daughter preparing breakfast. The mother was making the Indian flatbread – baked on an iron griddle and then toasted on the coals. The tea was ready on the back of the fireplace. The girl had one egg with which to make an Indian omelet. When all was ready, I watched the girl give the largest share to her father and me. Then she divided the rest among her 4 smaller brothers. That one egg served 6 people. All of us were satisfied as we finished off with our bread and hot tea.

"It is more blessed to give than to receive."
(Deuteronomy 15:7)

According to this verse the blessing is to the giver. True. However, a gift given in love, small or great, lingers on in the memory of the receiver as well. Through the years I have received many beautiful and useful gifts, but there are three that stand out in my memory. All of them were from children.

It was my commissioning night at First Baptist in Minneapolis, and I would be leaving for India very soon (1945). My friends presented me with a love gift. After the meeting was over, Dave, from the junior high Christian Endeavor Group I had been leading, came up to give me a fistful of pennies. He would not put them in the offering plate; for he wanted to be sure I got that parting gift. I have never forgotten.

On my first furlough I stayed in the home of a dear friend. It was just after Christmas and Jim, her 6 year old son, had received a hammer for Christmas. Not just an ordinary hammer for into the end of the handle was a set of small screw drivers, one within another. I was intrigued and mentioned how useful that would be in India. Later I saw Jim whispering to his father. His father nodded and then Kim gave his little hammer to me. Yes, I used it for 38 years in India and I still treasure it. One of the most precious gifts I have ever received.

On another furlough I was a guest at a small church in Minneapolis. After the service there was a meal. As I sat at the table, Betty, maybe 10 or so, came up to give me a lovely yellow rose from their garden. I was very touched.

Why do I remember these three gifts so well? It is because with each gift, the giver gave something of himself/herself. It is more blessed to give then to receive, but that blessing carries over to the receiver as well.

"For unto to you a child is born."
(Luke 2:11)

We pulled into a tiny Kurku village late one afternoon. I've long since forgotten the name of that village; we all call it Bethlehem. We were a group of Christians – one American, three Indian ladies, two Indian evangelists, and a young boy. We usually put up tents and stay overnight. We were all weary for we had been on tour for some time. The men didn't want to put up the tents so we enquired about a vacant house. Yes, the villagers gladly led us to a tiny room. The floor had been freshly smeared with manure and mud and a woman was already vigorously sweeping, moving the dust from one place to another. It looked clean so we decided to use it even though it meant the men would have to sleep out on the veranda.

The trailer was unloaded and all the baggage stacked in the middle of the room. Then the men went off to get the water and we women began sorting out the tin trunks and the bedding, preparing to cook the evening meal. The men returned somewhat disgruntled for the water they brought for drinking and cooking purposes was of a greenish hue and smelled. They had driven the buffalo away from the pool in order to get that water. There was no well in the village. We ladies were weeping. The wood we had was wet and smoke filled the room making our eyes smart and burn. No one was pleased with Bethlehem.

After the evening meal our spirits rose, and we went off to the village to hold our evening meeting. Much later we returned to our house, spread our bedding out on the floor, and prepared to sleep. We were so tired and it felt so good to stretch out, but now as we got down on the mud floor we knew we were in a stable. The odor was so strong that no one could sleep. And now we heard the animals we had displaced. They were just on the other side of the bamboo matting, and that matting was not exactly sound proof. The large bells of the buffalo, the middle-sized bells of the cattle, and the tiny bells of the goats clanged and tinkled all night. Sleep was impossible.

Then some of the ticks began leaving their former hosts to feast on us. Now the bite of these ticks itches for days and none of us liked to have them crawling on us. I really can't vouch for the thoughts of the Indian ladies, but I do know what was going through the American's head. I was thinking of my comfortable home back in the States and wondering how I ever got into such a situation.

Then I heard a voice, and, recognizing it, whispered, "Are You here too Lord?" "Yes," came the answer, "I have been in a stable before. I came to Bethlehem – remember? You just left North Dakota, but I left Glory. I laid aside equality with the Father to come to Bethlehem." The Lord of Glory in a stable! The Creator, a babe at Bethlehem! And I bowed in that smelly stable to worship and adore the Lord who so loved the world that He was willing to live with sinners in order that He might die for sinners, that He might reconcile us unto God.

And now it is Christmas again here in America – all over the world. Let us come humbly to Bethlehem acknowledging Jesus Christ as Lord of our life, and like the wise men of old let us present our gift – a life wholly devoted to His service.

> *"Behold I am going to do something in your days that you would not believe even if you were told."*
> *(Habakkuk 1:5)*

This was the promise God gave me one morning in 1976 as I prayed for help – for missionaries to reach the Korkus.

And they came – missionaries not from America, but from India! From South India the Church Growth Mission sent two couples. They did not stay long, but one couple led a young man to the Lord. His name was Ganeshpande.

From Mizoram the Zoram Baptist Mission sent two couples. They also worked hard without seeing much fruit. One man died and the other couple was called back to Misoram. They were replaced, however by five new couples.

Then young people from the Evangelical Mission of India came into the area where Ruth (Ihrig) and I first began to witness to the Korkus. Among them was Ganeshpande who returned to witness to the Kurkus.

This past January and February I returned to that area and began revisiting the villages I had known so well, going over the same horrible roads in the same old jeep I had used in 1982!

Letters From India

True to His work, I could hardly believe what I was seeing... small groups of believers gathered to greet me with garlands, gifts, and of course food and tea. They were using the Korku translations and song book I worked on for so many years.

In one area I revisited, three of the evangelists were the young people I had worked with when I was there as a missionary. Rambhau, a run-away teenager, who finally became my helper in translation, is now the evangelist/pastor of the largest group of Korku believers. I could hardly believe my eyes!

I returned to Minneapolis rejoicing that our work and your prayers and financial help all through the years (1945-1982) was not in vain.

Written after retirement

Editor's Note:

Beryl was asked to travel to India with a group of international students whom she taught and fellow teachers as their interpreter. It was ten years or so after her retirement (we have never been able to verify the date although we have a picture of the group in India.) It was a great joy for her to visit her India home and see the changes because of her ministry there.

Wherever she went the entire village came out to welcome her with flowers, gifts and cups of tea.

Chapter 9
Fruits of the Spirit

"Papa she is our grate grandmother is it?"
(Baby Beryl)

(Because the copy of this letter was very frail, I wasn't able to copy the original into the manuscript, however it was transcribed exactly as written.)

Dear Dadi *(Grandmother)*,

Greetings in the name of our Lord and Saviour, Jesus Christ. I beg your pardon for writing you after long time. Please forgive me. Thank you for your letter. May God bless you in this new year. We are praying everyday for you with the hostel children. The situation at our hostel is good. I am sending you a photograph of our hostel children with our church members.

At present the man of God helping me time to time for our hostel ministry with clothes and with some financial support. But that is not in regular basis. I am thankful to the Lord because God is so gracious to us because of your prayer support. As I wrote last time that we have eleven girls and nine boys. And we are running the hostel by faith.

But sometime we have to cry to the Lord for single meal to set before the children. But God never allow our children to sleep without food. And thus is the greatest testimony for the Dharni people. Pray that God may open the door for us. Maybe by next few month we will be registered. Then our hostel's name will be "BERYL GIRARD" Boys and Girls Home.

Again I am thinking to start an English medium school to support our orphanage and to support our ministry. We want to reach out every single Korku with the word of God. For that we need more evangelists and missionaries. We don't have proper support, but we want to support ourselves through English Medium School. So please pray for us, so that we may able to start the English Medium School.

In future we are going to have (1) Beryl Girard Boys and Girls Home, (2) Beryl Girard English Medium School, (3) Beryl Girard Training Center for Pastors and Evangelists. I will be glad if we can start our goal within this two years.

My daddy, Rambhau Kaka and his families doing well. But I haven't see Bapurau these days. But he is doing well. My second daughter also doing good. At present my wife looking after the hostel. Also I am looking at Rehatya Village Church (beyond Tapta River). Pray that somebody may come and help me in taking care of this house prayer groups. I will write in detail in next letter.

Dadi, how you are? Are you doing good? How about your knee problems? Is there somebody in charge to take care of you? We (our family, church, members, hostel childrens) pray everyday for you.

Baby Beryl and Irwin love to see your photo and remembered you by saying, "Papa, she is our grate grandmother, is it?" They love to listen about your ministry which is you have done in this area.

May God bless you Dadi, we love you so much. Please greet everybody whom you know.

With Prayer and love,

Your son in Christ, Lalsingh

Editor's Notes:

B.A., Beryl's brother, once asked Beryl if she had a chance to do it all again, what would she have done differently? She replied, "I would have gone to medical school, think of what I could have done!"

Later in life as Beryl and Al were waiting for her doctor, she told Al she wished she could have done more. Al said, "But Beryl, think of what you did do!"

Chapter 10
The Final Journey

"For What Is Seen Is Temporary, But What is Unseen is Eternal"

(2 Corinthians 4:18b)

Beryl died on March 15, 2008, in the presence of loved ones, and thanks to Al and Shirl's continual care, pain free and at peace. Her funeral was attended by students of her Bible Study classes, her international students, her English as a Second Language classes, her supporters, fellow parishioners, members of the clergy and family.

Al was executor of her meager belongings and what little money remained. She gave to whoever asked for her help. Al notified her countless friends of her death. Letters of condolences and stories of her were received from all over the world.

She was buried near the farm on which she spent her early years, next to her mother and father, and became once again, a part of the North Dakota prairie she loved so well.

§§§

Pam Girard has written two cookbooks on easy cooking, *If It Tastes Good, Who Cares?* and *If It Tastes Good, Who Cares?, II*. Recipes from her books have appeared in *"The Best of the Best from the Great Plains Cookbook, 1999, Best of the Best Recipe Hall of Fame Quick and Easy Cookbook, 2001,* and *The Recipe Hall of Fame Cookbook, II, 2003*. Pam's recipes evolved from her classes on easy cooking.

During 1994, her column, "Easy Cooking" appeared in the Bismark Tribune.

She has traveled extensively and began giving lectures on "Traveling the World Solo", "Traveling the World with a Carry-on", and "How to Pack."

Presently she is working on a third cookbook on easy cooking and the book, *Being Hungry in Tibet* and other stories of her travels is in the planning stages.

She resides in Bismark, North Dakota.